Candle in the Wind

A Brokenhearted Memoir Of My Hero

AUSTINE ARNOLD

Candle in the Wind
A Broken-Hearted memoir of my Hero

Published by:

Austine Arnold.

Facebook: Austine Arnold
Twitter: @arnoldaustine
LinkedIn: Austine Arnold
Email: omondiwere01@gmail.com

Cover Design and Layout by:

CORE MEDIA

Email: info@coremedia.co.ke

Twitter: @mwanamwenga

ISBN: 978-9914-703-29-0

Candle in the Wind

To the love of my life,

My dearest mother,

Joan Auma Keya

I commit to forever
take care of you.

Candle in the Wind

To the finest friend of my youth,

My friend for all seasons,

Theodore Mark Juma

I owe you a fortune, and
I intend to pay it back.

Candle in the Wind

Candle in the Wind

'Your candle burned out long
before your legend ever did'

Elton John,
Candle in the Wind

$$\text{❧} \diamond \text{❧}$$

Candle in the Wind

Contents

Candle in the Wind

Prologue

"I miss sharing a history

I miss looking forward to a shared future

I miss assuming there is all the time in the world.

I miss believing the best is always yet to come"

Carla Malden
AFTER IMAGE

My grandmother broke my heart. It is the punch you do not expect that knocks you out. I sat down to write this preface the evening she passed on. Her death really broke my heart because she had chosen to do us dirty by dying right in the middle of the Corona Virus disaster that was plaguing the world. I had really wanted to go see her when her sickness had exacerbated but I had hit a dead end with that because of the reason abovementioned. I surely hope she died in peace and stillness because I had felt extremely sorry for her from what my mother told me her last days looked like: she seemed in unimaginable pain and trauma.

I had certainly been feeling sorry for her in her sunset years. She had lost the doting love of her life, her favorite brother and her most beloved son all in a span of six months. In the three years she lived after that, she was often alone, lonely and sickly. We shuttled her from one hospital to another and she always asked me why death was forgetting about her all the damn time it came around the block. I always told her she was going nowhere, not before I paid my dues to her.

What really made her demise a breaking point for me though was because I had let her down on the one undertaking she had constantly badgered me on; as if that were her dying wish. She wanted me to marry and we had agreed that April was the last deadline she was giving me to bring my wife home. I know how it really mattered to her that she dies once I am settled. April came, and with it a global pandemic as if on cue.

I was saved by an invisible hand once more. One year earlier she had pushed me to the wall and I had assured her that I had bagged myself a very beautiful girl from Sega and I would be presenting her without any further delay. She asked to talk to her on phone but I put my foot down that I wanted them to meet face to face first.

When I failed to do so over the December festivities, I was given the final extension that would lapse over Easter. She pointed to me the cock she would be keeping to prepare for her and so there was no escaping this time round.

As April began, I had in point of fact decided to travel home to spend some time with my mother over the pandemic because things were slow and schools were closed but then a cessation of movement in and out of Nairobi was declared by the President the very day I was to make the drive home and that plan went up in smoky flames. I was stuck at the capital.

A fortnight later, I remember getting the depressing call from my mum that Mama Maria had gotten quite sick she could neither walk nor have a straight conversation. The first time my mother told me that, I told her I would sneak out of Nairobi immediately to go spend some time with her in hospital. She advised me against it and I also knew it was going to be a tall order because my driving license had expired and there were roadblocks all over the highway stretch to keep the viral pandemic at bay. I would have really loved to spend some time with her on her last days before she coasted away. It would have given me so much peace because I adored Maria so much: she lived her life with such grace, poise and flair.

Like with my father's demise, I harbor so much pain over

her death. I do not know much about fate as I write in this book but I know life happens to us all. Life knocks us over even when we are already down, sometimes especially when we are already down. I am always awed by that quote that says man plans and God laughs because sometimes I wonder if tragedy is God laughing at our plans. I do not know why my family has had to endure the pain of losing three of its most valuable people in the short span of three years. I cannot explain why that would happen to us and why God would expect us to be able to manage that great deal of pain. We remain forever scarred as a family steeped in great grief.

When my father died, I did not believe I was ever going to make it past that dark day. I had my heart broken to little pieces that day and I never thought I would be able to pick those pieces from the floor and ever piece them back together. And then I began to live every single day at a time from that day. Some of the days I went through without any much as a two minute beautiful memory of him while on other days I was on the literal end of the proverbial tether. Some days I made it out of bed and went to work and on some days I closed myself in for days on end only to be dragged out by my gracious therapist Emma. The first year was the toughest and every year after that it got a little better holding onto the grief. I always remember the enduring advice by my friend Elvince Ager that my father would be the only thing on my mind for a long time until his memory would nolonger be a reason for melancholy. Not a single day goes by without a memory of Japuonj, and yet today the bad days are in the negligible minority.

I loved my father immensely. He was the one man I looked up to for everything I wanted to achieve in my life. He was my true North. He was the compass direction the entire family relied on. He was my friend. In the few years before his death, we were very clearly heading towards being the best of friends but that was never to happen. I love the relationship we had over the years after several years of fearing him as a child. I know he deeply respected me as I grew into a man and he loved me as his son. He told me as much. My father never once told me how to live my life: he just lived his life and let me watch it and learn. I lived my life wanting to make him proud of me and I know for a fact nothing else would have mattered if he were still alive. I do not doubt that he continues to be proud of me from wherever he is because he does not stop being my true North. I hope he looks down upon his family and continues to guide it to the end of the pole.

I write this book to try and find the course of my grief over the years that followed: to know what tributaries it branched into and what main river it has finally spilled into and seemingly got a stable flow. This book is me attempting to give shape to what I felt when I lost my grandfather and then father and then a grandmother I constantly fawned over. It is an attempt to grieve openly

and to particularly keep little pieces of my father alive even in his death. I do not doubt that whenever this story is read, my father continues to live for eternity. He was a great man, as you will realize from this book, and I hope through this book I do justice keeping his legend alive. I share this with the world because I know I nolonger have to wrestle with the grief anymore: I can have it sit right by my side as a companion as we do life and keep honoring a wonderful wonderful man.

This is for you Japuonj.

My Father is Dead

11:44 am.
23rd March 2017.
Thomas Omondi Were.

His last breath was not a loud gasp. It was not a convulsive, deep and final pant either. He just did not struggle to draw in air anymore. He was not huffing or wheezing. He was, in the outright defiance of all expectations, collected in his reedy shape and quietly dying on his own terms. Only his eyes darted animatedly: perusing the white hospital ceiling that blocked the beauty of the undressed morning sky. There was no discernible or any uncontrollable shaking. He was not even having a fit as

I firmly held onto his hands, hoping against crumbs of hope that he would make it another second; minute; hour; day.

Here was a man shattering my entire abstract picture of a dying person: how they all go with a fight - squirming and screaming - clutching at straws in despondence: trying to fight the monster that is death. Trying to savor just one more second of this life. I always assumed nobody surrendered to death. I believed it ended with a fierce fight to live on and that even though death certainly had its way in the end, nobody ever gave in way too easily. I believed there was a script to death. I assumed there were telltale signs when death was nigh, and I supposed quietude was not one of the signs of a dying man. Nobody could possibly give in to death with the calmness of a yogi. Surely, death had to be just like any other opponent in the boxing ring: to be fought the full twelve rounds to the end of the rope unless it knocked you out along the way.

My dad, he just slept on his right hand and calmly let in death into the room to take over. In retrospect, it even looked like he invited it into the room. In his last moments, he freely handed the grim reaper the surrender baton: akin to that athletes give their fellows when they are done with their part in a relay. In his case, it did look like a clear admission of defeat. I imagine if he was on the battlefront, he would be the enormously worn-out soldier being riddled by the enemy bullets as he simply watched his body being butchered, doing nothing, waving goodbye to his compadres.

Only, we were the compadres here.

There is no point I can say with certainty that I saw him slip away. He just stayed still and drifted away in the silence of the morning hum. Still, then away. Away, then still. His eyes were wide open. He was breathing through an oxygen mask that had been fitted just that morning when he seemed to be fast losing breath. Like Leonard Cohen had said at his lowest point, my father had been a spectre of contradictions that morning: he was dying and yet he was not dying at that very same moment. Every second I thought he had slipped away, he would surprise me with one long draw in of air. It is that draw that continually assured me he was still alive.

A long and heavy draw.

It was such a cumbersome inhalation process that I will live the rest of my life unable to comprehend the amount of strength he needed to muster every time he made the draw in. He was clearly in great pain by that time. I live my life believing that every one of his last agonizing breath was a struggle to give us a few more minutes with him. I want to believe everything he did in those last moments, he did for us. Japuonj had been a man who had lived the most of his life for other people: for us especially. In his worst moment, he had never wanted us to panic. I know he wanted us to sort of transition in a smooth way when he let go.

Then, he let go.

I do not know the moment he coasted away right in front of me, unable to float back, unable to draw in more air. I do not know the exact moment Japuonj slipped away and yet I was right next to him holding his hands. I would like to live my life believing he did not want me to know. Like he had led his life for fifty three years, my father peacefully crept away into the world yonder. He made no fuss about it. He did it like it mattered not: just another life event, he must have deemed it. Like death was not such a big deal after all. Like those of us who were busy camping at his death bed, fervently praying, were flogging a dead horse.

How a man lives his life is his business, as Don Corleone famously quips in The Godfather, but I would come to learn that how he dies could be his goddamn business too.

Nonetheless, I still hold it against him that he would have at least given me a sign, any sign, even with a final gasp for air: a loud I-am-now-dying gasp for air. I think death is such a monumental event that one cannot slither away from like a wasted roisterer leaving a party in the dead of the night. It is not someone walking away from the dinner table after supper to reappear for breakfast the next morning. There is no coming back from death, because it is an event of far-reaching

proportions. It is an end in itself and I think ends deserve proper announcements. I think ends deserve proper announcements.

A whole journey of life stops at that very moment.

But, my father, he just died like an old Sicilian gangsta.

In our twist of fate therefore, there was no goodbye moment with my dad on his death. No silent farewell that I can look back at every time with great nostalgia; not a particular moment to clutch onto for the rest of my life and reminisce about. Until this day, I find it very difficult to explain to anybody the exact moment my father died. In his life, I remember my father had never been good at farewells and people would notice he was gone long after he had bolted out of the scene. Turns out even on his death-bed the man still saw no point in farewells. Morbid Gangsta, Japuonj.

I had never been by anybody's bed side as they died, but the little I had gathered from books, film and whatnot had made me believe there were always farewells. That there was always that time somebody submitted that they could not do it anymore and 'goodbye-ed' his people. That moment when they called their families around their bedside and gave them that last speech and an own tribute, attempting to give them closure: attempting to cushion the grief that was about to envelope them. Some sort of a montage of that very last moment when all of their life flashed before their very eyes. I could not have been quite wrong when it came to my father and futile farewells.

Later on, it is something that I would see with Bob Collymore, the enigmatic Safaricom Chief Executive, who would even go on to organize his wake to the last detail once he had realized there was no way out of his Acute Leukemia. Knowing he was dying and having tried all manner of ways to save his life, Mr. Collymore would surrender to the reality of death and even host his best of friends for a final wake with expensive Single Malt and ask them to allow him fly to paradise. He knew his story was done, and he wanted to waltz out of this earth on his terms and so he did. For Mr. Collymore, I cannot imagine the amount of strength he had to muster but I for sure believe he gave the supporting cast around his life some level of closure. That is what I had expected from my old man.

I would also see it with the inimitable Kibra Member of Parliament Kenneth Okoth who would tell his wife 'let me go" when the pain of Cancer became unbearable at the Nairobi Hospital. He saw it come and knew he would never want to be under the yoke of pain forever and so he let go and asked his people to do the same. He had actually been undergoing Cancer treatment abroad and when he saw no hope yonder, he made peace with it and decided to come back home. A similar

thing transpired with the then Bomet Governor Joyce Laboso who would tell his family 'I want to go home now' before she took a bow, unfortunately her demise also occasioned by the scourge of Cancer. This was the script I always knew. This was the script I was expecting to play out in my case too.

Not with Thomas Omondi Were.

Not Japuonj.

I had been seated by his bed side all along, clasping his ice cold left hand that held their wedding ring that he had worn since their beautiful wedding with my mother in August 1998. I had never seen him without it. I was holding onto his hands tightly as if to assure him everything was going to be fine despite how bleak everything looked at that very moment. With every passing instant, I had been fastening my grip as I loudly sang to him the first two stanzas of Robin Mark's timeless lovely hymn:

'I Will Sing The Wondrous Story".

'I will sing the wondrous story
Of the Christ Who died for me
How He left His home in glory
For the cross of Calvary.

> Refrain:
> Yes, I'll sing the wondrous story
> Of the Christ Who died for me

Sing it with the saints in glory
Gathered by the crystal sea.

I was lost, but Jesus found me
Found the sheep that went astray
Threw His loving arms around me
Drew me back into His way.

In retrospect, I do not believe I was singing with the hurricane of emotions that was washing through me. If you know me I know you may not quite believe it too, but I was singing that song so piercingly in that instant. All I know is that the height of my desperation in that moment allowed me to do anything for my father as he died. I went all out singing and humming to him as I held his hands as if he was a small baby asking for a lullaby in order to sleep. I only knew the hymn refrain and the first two stanzas of the hymn, so that's what I had been going over, for over two hours as he coasted away. It was the only hymn I had two stanzas off the top of my head. I rarely go to church neither do I sing hymnals while doing house chores and so even remembering that small bit was a herculean task.

The regulars in church that I had been expecting to sing to my father as he died were hunkered at the outside grass lawn of Aga Khan Hospital Kisumu, mourning a man still breathing. By that morning, in one sweeping look, they had all written him off and in hushed tones would peep back and ask each other if he was still

breathing. They were getting on my nerves. Everybody was getting on my nerves in that moment, and singing that song to my old man really pacified my broken soul. That was why I kept holding onto tiny morsels of hope despite the irritation with the people who were waiting for the go ahead to begin wailing: a go ahead that would come sooner than I expected. I understood them but I hated them quite a bit at that minute.

Here I was, taking a huge one for the team. If you indulge those who know me, they will tell you I cannot sing if it meant saving my life. I do not get allowed to sing in public places thanks to a greatly croaking and lousy voice. I was hounded out of the Maranda High School choir by my buddy, then choir leader, Dick Okite, for not having any sort of rhythm. Any time I begin to sing along to a song, my friends turn their gaze with great displeasure and I know it's time to stop with the croaking. I usually only take my voice to those Nairobi Karaoke shindigs where everybody has a croaking voice they do not even notice it. It's the only space my voice is acceptable at. And by the time the karaoke takes heat, people are normally too inebriated to notice there is a frog croaking to 'No One Like You' by P-Square on the makeshift stage.

But I told myself at that moment that if my father needed me to serenade him, I was going to do just that. I was going to sing to this man as life seeped out of him, and I was going to sing like it mattered not; because it really mattered not at that moment. So I regurgitated the one

hymn I knew to him as life slowly filtered out of his heart. I have grown up knowing that singing to a dying person gave them the peaceful transition they needed to the world beyond, or at least seen in those movies where they talk about death with such romanticized glory. It was the only thing you could do to a dying man: sing to them about heaven, about love, about paradise. Talk to them about the glory and joy of heaven. So I was giving Daddy the surreal transition he needed most at that time. In retrospect, I did not think about it like that on that day. I was just singing because it is all I was able to do at that moment of intense helplessness.

A day earlier, the resident parish priest of Milimani area in Kisumu had administered to him the Catholic sacrament of anointing the sick, anointing him with the olive oil for his final journey, known to the church as extreme unction. Practicing Catholics refuse to acknowledge that this oil is normally only offered to the terminally sick, because it is always only on very rare circumstances when it is administered. I am glad my father got the anointing nonetheless because I saw how he got much more at peace after it. I however knew my mother had called on the priest to come and do the anointing because she sort of knew the ship had long sailed. The horses had long bolted out of the stable. His looming death was a fait accompli to her by that time.

As I continued humming and singing as if in and out of a trance, I did notice at some point the irregular drawing in of air had now completely fizzled out. His hands were getting icy, and his body was now becoming quite stiff. His mouth and eyes were still open: the lips as dry as dead skin and the eyes way watery by now. He just slept on the bed, calm and not moving any part of the body. Everything had become eerily tranquil. I panicked. I felt a sharp sting through my body at that point and an unusual corrosion in my stomach. He must be dead! Oh shit he is dead!

I unfastened my grip on his now taut fingers and passed my hands on his distended neck artery. Naught. There was no movement. I remember touching my neck artery at that moment and doing a comparison of sorts. What followed was a moment of glorious confusion as I quickly called Helen (our attendant nurse) who came in with the pulse recording kit, to see if there was any life japuonj was still probably harboring. I took a quick glimpse of the device she was using even as she tried to hide it.

Pulse 0, it read.

Nothing.

I managed to voice a frail −Hey, its fine if he is already dead- but she was insistent on calling in a doctor to 'declare him dead'. Professional ethics, she whispered to me, muzzling her very own tears, something she wasn't succeeding at. She had grown attached to Daddy, yet she was merely just the lady who brought him drugs

and gave him injections. She had only known Thomas (as they fondly called him) for ten days. Here I was, his son for twenty four solid years, staring at his lifeless body about to be covered by a long white sheet and thrown into a cold mortuary cement slab. And there was his wife of over 30 years about to enter the cubicle and find the love of her life a gone conclusion.

I was lounging on the brink of a precipice. There was no yonder to look at.

How would there be anything without Daddy? After twenty four years, how had a great man like my father gone down the hole that simply? How? In that split second, I was breaking real quick. And I was breaking down really fast because everything was coming back to me in a flash: our whole lives together as a family. I could not comprehend what was going to happen if my father passed away and how vulnerable he was going to leave us as a family. We were losing our lynchpin. We were losing our compass direction and there was no telling what sort of direction the family was going to take thereafter. Why had God chosen us? Why had God picked us, really?

My father had been the strongman of our family, and as he lay there dying, everything looked so bleak despite how reassuring my mother had tried to be over that period. Our brightest star had gone out with a mere flicker and the pain that was going to follow would

be Armageddon. I could not imagine how we were supposed to move forward with our lives. I could not imagine if there was ever going to be a future in the first place without my father. I knew for a fact that there was no way I was even going to make it past that day. Why did I need to? I for sure knew I did not have to.

On those days that it grew really imminent that japuonj was dying, I remember how we took turns with my mother sleeping on the floor at the hospital that gave no thought to a caretaker, only providing a single plastic chair. We had one shawl and we both used it differently. Her, she slept on the cold hard floor and covered herself with the shawl saying she could sleep anywhere as long as she covered herself. Myself, I spread the shawl on the floor, slept on it and inserted my fingers on my T-shirt and let my time tick away. We always had a two hour shift agreement, an agreement which my mother always flouted but always woke me up when my time immediately lapsed. Sometimes during the day, she took time to really reassure me that we were going to make it on our own, that God would not let something happen to us that we could not handle. But most of the times in the night, we took turns crying hoping nobody else saw our vulnerability: not even each other. The defenselessness my father faced at that moment is a heartbreak still clogged at my chest. Nobody deserves to go through the level of pain and indignity that he went through on those last days.

Not a single soul should die the way my father did.

The doctor who was brought in to officially declare the death was a pretty, short-haired, bespectacled young lady. From all the pointers, she had not seen better days as a doctor as she got swept by a stinging sensation when she gave Daddy one look. After the cavalier attitude I felt I had seen with the doctor who had handled Daddy throughout our stay in hospital, I felt this lady would have given him more days had she seen him earlier. I wanted us to start afresh with her. I wanted to ask her her name and if she would take care of my father. I wanted to know her area of specialization. I wanted her to tell us if she knew his condition and if she would direct us to a better doctor. I also wanted to tell her maybe she was too late to the party. In the end, I told her nothing.

She too, muzzled her tears and I actually came to re-learn at that moment that doctors were not robots after all. At least not this pretty, short-haired, bespectacled young doctor who fate was befalling to declare a man she did not know as dead. A man the first time she was seeing was a mound of a stiff ice-cold body. She had begun by steadily removing the oxygen mask and attempting to look at his vitals when I noticed she wanted to skirt around matters and rudely interrupted her.

'Is he dead Daktari?"

"His pulse has been low like you may have been told in the morning and the organs have been fast deteriorating..."

{Interrupted again}

"Is he dead Doc?"

"I .... am .... sorry ....but "

"Let's have a few moments with him before he is towed away to the mortuary"

In a few moments after the pronouncement, my mother peeked into the curtains from outside the cubicle.

My father is dead, I shouted back at her.

She began singing: Let the Lord have His Way.

11:45 am.
23rd March 2017.
Thomas Omondi Were.

The man we had all - including our mother - fondly referred to as daddy would be declared dead.

Gone with the Wind.

I remember the flurry of questions that kept going through my mind at that moment as I stood by his bedside looking at him restlessly. What are we going to do now without you Daddy? Is this real? Are you seriously, really dead? Is this how people die? Why did it have to end this way for you Daddy? What will we even be without you Daddy? What am I without you? Why did you not wait and see me amount to something first? Where did you get the Cancer they are suspecting you could have died of? What is wrong with you? How do you want my mother and your mother to live without you? What is life even worth now? What have you done to us? You really could not let us even mourn your own father well? Do you want my mother to follow you? How about your own mother? What killed you? Who killed you? Why did they kill you? Are you happy now that you have died and left us all alone? Are you happy now that you have died and left us all alone? Are you happy now that you have died and left us all alone? Tell me, are you?

> I do not want to live anymore. I cannot live anymore without you, man.

I was conflicted and confused. Having spent the whole time with him in hospital, I could not say that at some point I had not seen this was a probable eventuality. I had seen it coming from a million miles away. His death was always lurking in the shadows. But you learn that there is the thought that someone is dying and then them actually dying. I was overcome by sadness, anger and denial all rolled into one. I was snowballing into my stages of grief and I was experiencing them all at once: well, apart from acceptance. I knew one way or another I did not want to continue living anymore because I had no father to make proud any longer.

There was no way this was happening to us. Just two hours earlier, our doctor had told us to gather around Daddy and wait for his time to die. My heart literally sank at that moment. Everybody can give up on you when you are looking dejected in your hospital bed, but when your doctor does there is no coming back from it. So at that moment I had told myself there was nothing more I could do: that my father had gotten to the end of his life story. This was it. My mother was telling the Lord to have His way with him. Then he died and I could not come to terms with it at that moment. Somehow, I had clutched onto some hope on the fringes: that we would still make it out of this. How sublime my thinking had been. I wanted to do everything for him. It is unnerving how you can want to do everything for someone and yet still not be able to do a single thing.

I remember Ian, my brother, opening the curtains to check in on him as he had been doing since morning and I blurted out a loud "He is dead" to him and he stood there like I was pulling his legs so I had to shout back one more time: "OSETHO". Looking back, I think that's the one way I was trying to deflect the conflicting emotions I was feeling in my heart in that instant. I took on the role of telling everybody who opened the curtain that the man they were coming to check on was already dead. Do not bother, he is gone, he is not coming back. Just join the rest in crying because japuonj is already dead in here. It was my own way of coming to terms with his death. I was throwing it to other people to hold it other than myself. I wanted everybody to deal with it apart from myself that minute. I threw it away from me like a professional rugby player does the rugger ball when the violent opponent is closing in.

I remember, once more, giving Daddy one sweeping look and asking myself:

So this is how it ends for you old gangsta? This is how you die? This is where the journey ends for you? This is it? You've got to be fucking kidding me man.

Goddammit Daddy!

11:44 am.
15th September 2016.
Michael Were Atogo.

Six minutes later, six months earlier, my father would calmly drive my grandfather into his boma in Masiro Konya to die: after five grueling months of running around with him trying to score treatment for his benign prostate enlargement: which would later morph into kidney nephritis and to prostate cancer which would eventually close the curtain of his life. A good man, my grandfather had been and it was sad how of all persons he met such a sad death. That time, I had learnt the burden of an ageing parent fell on the son. My father

took up the duty of caring for his father like it was his other calling besides teaching Mathematics. It was quite the sad spectre to watch him struggle to get his father back on his feet.

I remember painfully informing myself during that period that cancer had finally managed to sneak backdoor into our family. My heart had been really heavy the first time my mother had suggested that Mzee could be having Prostate Cancer. I had until then made the erroneous assumption that cancer was a disease that belonged to other people and not us. I did not even have an idea how any form of Cancer manifested itself until that moment when my mother had opened that Pandoras box. We were supposed to be a cancer free family. We were supposed to be the children of the greater God.

My father, in his usual fashion of protecting everybody else and taking the hit himself, had deflected the imminent death of my grandfather with a lot of medical language on cell sizes, symptoms and whatnot. He was not sure if there was any medical emergency, he would always conclude. Mzee was extremely sick, that is all he would say when you cornered him for an explanation. I surmised that he was always being creative with the facts. He was going to be fine and back to his feet in no minute, he was always keen to add. I always believed him until my mother presented a different set of facts. And then I believed that new set of facts.

A day to his death though, he would give up the information on what was ailing Mzee. He would tell me how cancer had finally managed to break his body and how he was in so much pain he actually deserved rest. Like every parent though, he would ask me not to worry, that an operation was scheduled and it would go on just fine and Jaduong' would be back to his feet in no time. I loved how he called him Mzee though: a really sharp contrast to how we called him Daddy. I knew that even with us there was always going to be a transition from calling him Daddy to Mzee at some point. He was always going to grow to be that old and it would only befit calling him Mzee then. Well, humor me. Man plans and God laughs.

During those five months in and out of hospital, my grandfather would surmount a great deal of pain. Cancer really assails you like a bulldozer razes a building: with unforgiving brute. It is taxing and unrelenting. It eats you up with the relish of a hungry lion that has killed a prey in the wild. In six months, it turned my healthy grandfather to a reedy shadow of his former rotund and healthy self. It showed him no mercy, ravaging him like a wild bulldog does a trespasser to the owners' property. His pictures on those last days are a sight you would hold your breath to because they depict excruciating pain by themselves. They are a perfect case of a picture speaking a thousand words by itself.

I had been offline that day and my mother would call me

later in the evening, while sipping tax-free beer with my campus buds at the KBC army canteen to casually tell me he is already dead. She had told me the day before that Mzee was in his last moments, but she was still holding onto morsels of hope. And I had told her he was dying, and that we were better off giving up. You are not God, she had chided. Now here she was telling me he was already dead. The word 'already' counted for everything in her statement: that she had been holding onto God for a miracle but she knew the set of facts on the ground were saddening. This was one of those instances when hope is a really long stretch.

On the morning my father died, she had told the doctor when her hope had reached the zenith: just let us be around him at this time, I just want to be with him, just leave him. That morning, unlike less than just a year before that, she never held on for an impossible grace like I did. She only sang her "Let the Lord have His Way" refrain.

He is already dead.

It did hit me, the death of my grandfather, but I would not be quite moved by the death of Mzee, because the previous day my father too would tell me he was on his way out, his days over. But that's not why I would not be greatly shattered by the passing on of a gracious grandfather we fondly called Kwara and everybody else called Mika. At 86 years old, and having visited him at a time when he was in immense pain, I had thought he needed to rest: and death, a grave, was the ultimate rest-dom at that age. It is the place of peace and quiet. It is the zone of stillness, of nothingness. At that age, even he used to tell us, there is not much he had not seen. You could not live in this world forever, he always added. But he had also been very casual with death: he saw it as nothing more than an end and he contended that every life had to come to an end at some juncture. I agreed with him at that time.

Not a year later though as my father died in Aga Khan Hospital, Bed 10.

Is there any of us who is going to come out of this life alive? Are you going to live forever? He often asked us when we sought his wisdom on mortality. A situation that would be repeated as my father died: he often told people who visited him that death was just a part of this life. If I should die, then that would be just how life works. People come, people go. I always just looked at him and I knew if he was a kid I would have hit him with a hockey bat for spewing such nonsense. What sort of nonsense. They possibly imagined their death did not have far reaching proportions. They have literally ground an entire family to a halt.

Death was just a normalcy to these two gentlemen.

My grandfather was an old man born in the 1930's to a large and extremely poor family, a situation that would make him have to drop out of school quite early in Primary Six. From then on, he did a lot of menial hand jobs, even being a quarry worker at some point of his life. Because of his level of education at the time, he would then go on to work as a clerk in different places such as the Kilindini Harbor until he would retire in 1986 and decide to move back home. By all standards, he was a man who had lived the proverbial humble life until the point of his death. He knew no largesse or posh-ness in the entirety of his life. He took care of a large family right to the last moment, without raising a complaint and yet with little income coming from planting sugarcane and selling to the Mumias Sugar Company. He was the emblematic father, and by all standards a model grandfather too. He was actually the only grandfather I had as my maternal grandfather had died twelve years before I was born.

It is in that same vein of humility therefore that he breathed his last in a mat in his mud-walled three-roomed house in his Masiro boma. Like he had lived his life, he went out with such self-effacement as he did grace. He was a good man, Mika and he died in the most exasperating of ways.

That evening as he had lost his father, I would lose any nerve to condole my father: because I did not know how to face a man who had seen his father die. I did not know how you get to tell a man 'sorry for losing your father'. I did not know how to talk to a man who had

lost his father. At that point I merely presumed it and I would come to know how hard it actually was. Later on, I would come to know losing a father breaks the camels' back for any man. It broke mine, and I bet it broke my fathers too despite how aged Mzee had been. I know he possibly had lost one of the people he loved most and it hit him hard too.

For both of us, I believe our fathers had been our brightest megastars. They had been the one man we turned to for inspiration on life, and for an ounce of wisdom. Like my father, my grandfather was a pensive fellow. He spent most of his time listening to his radio, as my pops spent his reading. He sat alone most of the time and toyed with his thoughts. He listened more than he spoke, and whenever he spoke, you got the sense of a man who calculated his words and who did not run his mouth. Both of them always managed to remain calm even in the direst of situations. Mika and his son were quite pedigree gents.

Those two sons of women were men that were greatly inspirational; men who walked into a room and you wanted to crowd around them just to sap into their wisdom. My father was a man that was well-regarded: the man I wanted to grow up into. He was my true North. He was the man who meant everything to me. He was the one man who lit up my path to greatness. I always told myself that I would be a great man if I turned out into just half the man my father was. I always knew

I was going to have him around forever and I was going to have all the time in the world to make him proud. Well, humor me again.

I had visited him at a time when Mzee was at the peak of his illness, and I could see he was looking really fatigued. I guess it came with looking at your old man wither away. I remember after several days in the hospital with Daddy everybody was asking why I was wasting away so fast. It probably came with seeing your brightest star lose his shine. I was so stressed out seeing my father that vulnerable. I worried myself sick at why that was happening to him of all people. I mostly cried myself to sleep. I cried so much in the shower I do not know what will make me cry that much again. But the Luo say piny agonda. The world can surprise you.

After several hours of back and forth with myself on that evening that Mzee would die, I would send him a weak text – "Hello Daddy, Sorry about Mzee.' and, characteristic of my father, he replied with an even weaker –"Its fine. His time had come". Classic Thomas Omondi Were. That was typical Japuonj. A case of emotions masked so deeply never to be let out into the world.

Only one week earlier, he had sent me a text:

"Mzee says he wants you to be a great okil (lawyer)".

There are things you do not forgive even God for. I will not forgive God for the deaths of those two fine gentlemen.

I long wrapped it in my head that God can forgive you for not forgiving Him. That God understands. That God should understand. And even if He doesn't, I still will not forgive Him. My father's death took me down a suicidal path: it took me to a dark corner where I constantly said I did not want to live anymore. I cannot live anymore without my father. It took me down a path of constant nightmares every night. It took me down the narrowest dark alley there can be in this world. I lost my closest friends and things I held very dear. I lost any will to live. I lost myself in the pendency of intense grief.

I remember how I began having very intense hallucinations and dreams a few weeks after his passing on. On some nights just a few weeks after he had passed on, he would walk up to me in the dead of the night and tell me he was lonely wherever he was and he wanted my mother to go be with him. He was asking me to allow him take her. He was always asking me for permission for one thing or another. On some nights, he told me it's me he wanted to go be with him, that there was really no essence to living this life. He always told me how he wanted me to do it. And yet on some nights, he came and just slept beside me. On some nights he came as two different people: his usual self and the frail man he had been in his last moment. On some nights, he was telling me that there are people who had killed him and we had to wage on war on them. On some nights, he just sat there and looked at me. On some nights he gave me life advice. On some nights... He fucking visited me almost every night after we buried him for almost the whole of that first year. I was constantly hitting things while walking because I was always daydreaming too. I had no will to live at all.

My father's death took me down a path of self-destruction and insanity: a period I didn't know who I was and what I wanted for my life anymore. I constantly told myself I did not want to live anymore without my father. I cannot live any more without my father. I did not have a reason to continue living. What was the need? I lost my best friend Brian because I was projecting my anger and frustrations towards him constantly. I lost people who meant a lot to me and who I felt had lost their worth in my eyes because they had not come to Masiro to help me bury my Pops. I had no interest in my career anymore and for a long while was not interested in getting a job or even going back to School. I moved back with my brother after a year and became a couch potato at his house only leaving when my friend Ricky called me to hangout or have a drink. I lost myself. I had no will to keep on living at all.

Life can nick you so bad you fail to see the hand of God at play. This was that point in my life. I did not see God, despite the church groups that came to see my father in hospital every day. They prayed and praised, sang and sang more again, and yet Daddy still got worse every day. Where was God hiding? How busy was he as my father painfully died in hospital? Were we then the proverbial children of a different lesser God? I saw no God on those days my father writhed in pain. God had deserted us.

I do not know how men should die. But my grandfather, in an old dirty floor mat, slipped away like a rabid dog - with his mouth open - in excruciating pain. Like a fucking rabid dog. A mongrel at best. The ones you find at the edge of the hedge, ten days later, stinking to the high heavens. And my father, with his eyes wide open and mouth dry as a desert and trembling like a lunatic, died a man deprived of any dignity this life could have offered him at his dying moment.

I do not know how men should not die. But good men deserve a turn of good at their last moment, I should suppose. My grandfather, and father, died in the most brutal of ways a man can die. And so did my jolly grandmother. You could argue that a man shot to shreds dies gravely off, but it would still not be as brutal as ten continuous days of extreme excruciating pain that my father endured and never for one second raised his tone to complain.

I find dragged pain brutal, as opposed to moments of pain before death. When you have to see yourself dying for ten days, you feel like the scum of the earth. You feel stripped naked of any dignity. In his moments of extreme vulnerability, I remember my father talked about death, how close it was, as if it was a premonition that constantly occurred to him.

"Death cannot be treated. If it's your turn, it's your turn.

But I am not dying any soon though. "

And then he died.

On the day we would bury Mzee, I would write on my Facebook timeline:

"We bury my favorite grandfather today. A graceful man, Wuod Agatha. For five painstaking months, as the old man battled Prostate Cancer, my father would be at his side. Taking him to hospital every other day, monitoring his diet, medication and condition. He basically saw his father wither away into the night and night into the day. When I visited Mzee a few months ago, he was pale and emaciated. But he was not a sad man. He did not die a sad man. He asked me to buy him a "madiaba" coke and he drank it to the last swallow. That would be the only thing that would get into his mouth on that day, and it broke my heart a coke was all I could offer a dying man. But it was my father who disheartened me. Pale, he too was. You could see watching his father die had taken a toll on him. Even the night before the old man died (when his memory had been erased) it would be my father with him. I don't know what happens when your father dies not knowing who you are anymore. "

Until my father would die, my hands clutching his, with no idea whatsoever who I fuckin' was. Until I would realize my grandfather's death had merely been a rehearsal on what my father would subject me to. Hold my beer, he had simply told my grandfather. On the day that he would die I would be so angry at him, because he would leave behind an extremely broken son, an emasculated boy who now had to grow up so fast. I do not know if my grandfather had left him a broken son.

But I remain profoundly inspired by the words of Anne Lamott that "If you haven't already, you will lose someone you can't live without, and your heart will be badly broken, and you never completely get over the loss of a deeply beloved person. But this is also good news. The person lives forever, in your broken heart that doesn't seal back up. And you come through, and you learn to dance with the banged up heart".

Grief, I've learned, is really just love that has no direction. It's all the love you want to constantly give but are unable to. All of that unspent love gathers in the corners of your eyes, the lump in your throat, and the hollow part of your chest. Grief is just love with no place to go. Grief is just love. And love is love.

I am learning to dance with my banged up heart despite the fact that I wake up every morning knowing that my father is dead, and that I can never forget the exact moment he was pronounced dead.

11:45 am.
23rd March 2017.
Thomas Omondi Were.

Out Of Time

In December 2016 at what time I went home for the festivities as I had made a habit every year since moving to Nairobi for college studies, I encountered a man so worn-out it was evident in his deep sunken eyes. He was constantly exhausted regardless of whether it was very early in the morning or smack in the middle of the day. He just sat on the sofa watching boring local TV programs: but mostly, just staring into the hoary ceiling. He always looked rudderless as he moved around the house beneath the radar as if not wanting to be noticed. You would know he was calling you only when you looked at him and saw him motioning. He barely spoke and hardly stood up from one spot once he sat down.

He was uncharacteristically detached, and you would have to ask him something more than once to get his attention since he was constantly in a trance. It was unlike him: my father was always the alert one and was straight up always aware of what was going on. He was a man with quite a discernible spring on his feet. But something was ostensibly weighing him down greatly. Something was wrong because that had not been the man we had all known for all our lives. It must be that he was hit by the loss of his father, we continually concluded. Surely a man who had just lost his true North would be expected to glide through certain motions of grief.

He said nothing other than the fact that he felt a little indisposed and he was quite sure it was the stomach ulcer reflex. Just a month earlier, his fish farm investment had gone down the drain. There had been zilch return on that investment despite the fact that had he had sunk so much money and time to that project. Vagabonds had stolen most of the fish and the big ones had eaten the rest because they were being underfed by the person he put in charge. My mother would repeatedly ask him if that was the cause of the stress that was giving him the ulcers. But I knew my father; he would not go into a business without knowing that there was a probability of the investment being a mere sunk cost. He understood the risk. In any case, just eight years earlier, his passion fruit business had gone down a similar drain.

Also, my brother had just left school despite a million shillings having gone to his parallel program school fees. Another sunk cost. That could be the other reason, my

mother contended. In a bid to comfort him, I remember how she was telling him that the money had sunk into an irretrievable cause, and there was a little he could do to alleviate the situation anymore. Ian was an adult who had decided on how he wanted to live his life, she added. She told him he had fulfilled his parental duty to the hilt. You are too old to have a last born son give you ulcers. Let the world teach him, she retorted.

He said he was fine, just a little sick.

The interesting deal with my dad is that he was an extremely guarded man. He was the quintessential Luo stuck-in-the-mud guy: he kept to himself and tucked all his thoughts away neatly. Made crucial moves but kept his cards only closest to his chest. Largely, it worked for him till the end. Until he was on his death bed, my mother surprisingly did not know that much about his personal details either. After 27 years of marriage, my mother would say that his guarded and secretive nature had helped her become so independent at life. So I think it worked for her too. I don't know though, it was their marriage and therefore their business what worked and what they feigned as working.

She did her thing: he did his thing.

They met at the middle, whenever there was a middle ground.

I think more like my father, I am a very private man but

I would not keep my wife in the dark because the post-modernist conception of a marriage seems to mean signing on to a union of sorts and unions shouldn't thrive on secrecy: except just for the necessary secrets like lying about running late. I hope if I should marry my life becomes an open secret to my wife. It however seems that in this age of social media, there is only so much you can tuck away before your wife hits you with a 'we need to talk' on a Sunday morning after breakfast. This is just a supposition though because I have no experience on marriage or even a proper long term relationship as I write this. I have no yearning to get into one at the moment. If it is to happen, so be it.

I remember three days to his passing on my mother had insisted that he divulges to us his P.I.N(s) and passwords in case anything was to happen. So he had stalled long enough for her to leave the cubicle and then blurted out to me random passwords. Only he could not remember his main phone P.I.N at all by that time. So he had told me aisulu and burst out in his signature roaring laughter, which had now greatly faded altogether with his now bottom of the barrel health. We ended up not recovering that phone PIN at all. I only managed to recover it several weeks after he had passed on and I realized there may have been a few things he would have loved to stay as his secrets and which he probably wanted to go to the grave with.

After his passing on, I would go on to also remember

that one time in early 2015 while having a random conversation with him at Sandton Palace Hotel when he was visiting in Nairobi, he would tell me he was seriously considering taking a funeral insurance cover at Sanlam and we would not be bothered when he passed on. He had just discovered an interesting Umash and APA Insurance partnership. The good guys at Umash Funeral Home would cater for everything when such an eventuality occurred. We would just sit and mourn. I told him it sounded like a good idea and we marveled at how the idea of insurance generally was noble but there was a lot of chicanery in the business occasioned by fraudsters. He assured me that he would take out the burial plan the next time he visited the city. ,

Yet that would be the only one time he would mention it in conversation to anybody. And I would be the only person he would tell about it, albeit just in passing conversation. He would go on to take the insurance cover and diligently pay the premiums but not talk about it with anybody else. But that conversation would stay with me because I knew my dad was a classic kusema na kutenda person and it is the first thing that would hit me when he passed on. You would however expect though that he would tell somebody about it because he was of course never going to bury himself.

Which is why when he passed on, I would mention it quite a number of times and yet it would be dismissed as mere bluff. But Omondi Were was not a man who lived on pitching a yarn. I have told you he was quite a stand-up guy. So you can imagine the surprise when a fortnight after his burial I found the original insurance policy documents amongst his folders. He had, after all, taken that insurance cover and remained guarded about it. Interestingly, he had taken the cover for my mother too, and failed to tell her about it. That was some really morbid shit even for a man of his legendary privacy.

That December that I was home, even as he was detached, he continually insisted that he was well and it was just that ulcer that continually troubled him. He would not accept that he was sick: and he did not want anybody to think that was the case. He was toughening it up. Looking back, for a man who had been the breastplate of our family, I realize he never wanted anybody to panic at that time: he was trying to remain the man he had been all along; the giver of all things and the receiver of none. He was our effortless leader of the tribe. Up until his death, my father was the man people ran to. I figure he never wanted to get to the point where he had to run to people and he actually passed away without having to, not even in the last moment when he was pissing on himself. Two days to his death, he asked me if we needed money for food in the house.

But I had been greatly worried that December. I was not used to seeing him that gray. He was in pain, and you could see it, but we were working with the ulcers theory that the doctors had said. I had asked them to go for a colonoscopy and endoscopy endlessly but they did not seem to take it as seriously as I was. They were taking chances with it, whatever it was.

In early January 2017 before going back to Nairobi I would help drive him (he did all the driving) to Aga Khan Kisumu for more treatment. I remember he had an appointment with a Dr. Ogutu at the Doctors Plaza at 12am. The doctor would turn up at 3pm and lump more ulcers drugs on him without any further checkup. By then, he had been seeing Dr. Ogutu for a while and he had expected he would be more diligent this time and look into his case with more gravity. He did not. He of course just wanted to make his money. I do not know him, but he is undoubtedly the man who began the chain of causation that killed my father. I do not blame him for misdiagnosis because everybody makes mistakes, but I blame him for doing so little for a man who needed so much from him. He has made me have so much hatred for doctors that I cannot possibly believe they give a fuck more than say a tailor who stays with your material for two months after an agreement to do so in one week. I find doctors as pathological in their approaches as I do people in my own legal profession.

My father would later say on his death bed: "...that man just wanted my money. He wasted me so bad I would pass him in the corridor without flinching. If I should die it is on him." I do not know what more he could have done as a Doctor. I nonetheless know he would have done better for this man had put his entire life on his hands. I do not put his cause of death on him but I know he let down a man who depended on him for everything. I know he failed to diligently take care of a man who was at the end of the tether and whose only salvation maybe depended purely on his acts of omission or commission. This is not to say I personally hold anything against him because I never even got the chance to meet him, but I know for a fact he let down my big man.

That New Year, I left home in mid-January to go and try starting my own life in Nairobi. I had just finished my undergraduate course but was going to have to wait for a whole year before I could graduate. It was going to be tough getting placement but I hoped I would begin making something out of my life having been a dependent all through. My father handed me twenty five thousand shillings and requested me to get a house and stay in with my brother. He also asked me to get a job and pay him back his money in five months. It was a debt because he had already done his duty of taking me to school, he jested. He also reminded me of how he had worked at several construction areas in Nairobi and done numerous menial jobs to make ends meet when he didn't have a job in Nairobi. My father seemed to have a lot of these struggle stories.

So I packed my bags and left for Nairobi.

During the whole month of February, my mother would

repeatedly call that our father was very sick and he was all alone at our Ugunja home. She was back at her work station and was not always able to go back home. I was busy looking for a job and so was Ian so we made promises that we would make time and go see him. Then my mother changed her tone and told us that we would regret our decision and it damn well hit me what she was saying. I do not remember making a mental note to go home immediately, but I did not know my mother to be alarmist. She seemed to shoot straight from the hip all the time. I knew then things were not getting any better.

Just six months earlier, she had called me and insisted I go visit my grandfather or I would regret my decision. I packed my bag that Saturday and went home and I am glad I did because the next month I was bumping into my grandfather he was already in a coffin. She did not want the same to happen for our father, I figured. Would she forgive herself if it did? Would I forgive myself if I did not listen to her? Wait, was this merely history repeating itself?

After a little nudging, we convinced Ian to go for the first shift as I kept looking for something to do with my life. A few days before my dad passed on, Ian would write a hearty blog titled Nursing My Father on his experience taking care of his old man making him shitty porridge and humongous Ugali that he would not touch and how he would struggle to drive or do other mundane tasks.

Ian also later writes an interesting story about my dad that I feel compelled to share on how macho my father had been: because he was always sure to remind us he had a black belt in Karate.

He writes:

'In the wake of the very first year when my father took over at a little-known school in Siaya County – Rang'ala Boys Secondary – as the Principal, succeeding a hugely popular man, the students went on strike. One night, at around 10 p.m. (I remember because it was just after the News and we had been sent away to bed so the adults could watch 'The Bold and the Beautiful') the students – about 50 of them, by my rough estimate – surrounded our house and started pelting us with stones. At first, we hid in the bedrooms but soon as a stone went through and hit my sister, we converged at the corridors – as we figured stones could not pass through the walls – and we waited for the tension to die down, all the while taking care not to shit our pants. But those boys were determined to pelt us for as long as they could. So my father went into his bedroom, wore a heavy grey jacket, picked up this monster torch that was so popular in those days, grabbed a big ass rungu, told us to stay in the corridors and walked out the door. Alone. Less than twenty minutes later and those boys were back in class and silence and peace had been restored and he came back. One old man with a torch and a rungu; against over fifty students armed with stones. Folks, you can't make this shit up.'

That was the man we all grew up knowing, not this vulnerable guy my mother was asking us to go nurse. As Ian would be home over that period, I would shoot him a text and ask him how the old man was. Bad, he would say and I would request him to stop being sensational like his mother. Bad was not a description I had ever thought would be used to describe Japuonj at any time in my lifetime.

Until the day my mother would call that they would be airlifting my father to Nairobi because his situation was very bad. Then I would know that the center could nolonger hold. Was my father really dying before I paid him back the loan he had given me to start life with? I thought to myself this nigga better not be running out of time.

In Law School, Health Law and Policy was a scream. It was one of those course units I had really anticipated taking. This was majorly because it gave the student the intellectual space to interrogate real life medical complexes and issues as they arose. I actually found the unit more intriguing than the movies I had watched on medico-legal complications. I also did it because my best friends, Brian and Theodore, were doing Medicine and were almost becoming medics and I did not want to always be the blank one when we met. I made sure to always tell them that if they dared be negligent they

would have me to deal with and I was not one to spare them.

The course unit dealt with life and death issues that needed not just a moralistic angling, but sometimes fiddling with legal aspects of what a medical decision meant in so far as the law was concerned. Most of the issues that were dealt with in medical law peaked great interest in students of health policy and medical disputes. I therefore happened to be a great fan of the subject. How should a doctor for instance decide who to treat first when approached by three different patients at the same time? If he makes a choice and the other patient dies, would there be a cause of action? What were the principles that a doctor had to adhere to while practicing medicine?

One other such medial complex was the issue of Euthanasia/Assisted Death/Mercy Killing/Assisted Suicide. This refers to the taking of a deliberate action with the express intention of ending a life to relieve a person of intractable, persistent and unstoppable suffering mostly with their consent. Bluntly, it is killing somebody to relieve them of the untold pain they are in. You can say it is taking the law in your hands to do good or bad depending on what side of your bread is buttered.

You can imagine how that presented a stimulating area of discussion.

Is it right? Is it moral? Is it legal? Is it necessary? Is it the easy way out?

So we tinkered with ideas in class on what school of thought and wavelength everybody was at. And it helped we were being tutored by a jovial Naomi Njuguna who made it an even more interesting discussion because she gave room for having a broad spectrum debate. Bless her soul, she is a good teacher that one.

People took sides real fast.

There are those who were flat-out against the idea and most of them had a religious angle in rejecting the idea. They held that because it is God who gives life to His creatures, then therefore it is only him who can take it when He deems fit. A human being has no power over the life of another human being. They were not willing to take the discussion above that and they quoted a whole lot of scripture to support their idea. Mostly, these were the extremely religious folk who tended to avoid any discussion that touched on the meta-physical aspects of the world. This group of students constantly argued that it was not in the space of man to touch on life because that was a sin that sent you directly to hell. Thou shall not kill, the commandments had very strictly ordered and there was no room for wiggling. They were not having any of this discussion and I actually remember one of them walking away from class in protest.

Then there are those who said it was only moral

and right to assist somebody to die when you were relieving them of untold suffering. Because what was it worth living without dignity? They even quoted the constitutional articles on dignity and a whole shebang of international instruments that buttressed human dignity as a sacrosanct human right. They went on to argue that dignity was one of the greatest requisites every human needed to be assured of, and because it was even guaranteed by our constitution it would be a travesty to deny one that right at the moment they needed it the most. So we needed to allow people to die with their dignity intact. We needed to stop being selfish over other people's lives and disregarding their anguish. Most of these were liberals who allowed room for independence of thought.

And there are those who never knew where they fell, they who just followed the discussion to learn from both sides and maybe make a decision at the end. The square pegs in round holes. Those who just followed ravishing the points either opposing sides presented and clapped or booed depending on the point that was made. This group of lukewarm students has always interested me because it is as if they mostly fear taking stands due to inferiority complexes. Why would you want to be a lawyer and still not have an opinion? Why would you be a human being and not have an opinion?

I stood for preserving the dignity of a dying soul. I held that it helped nobody seeing somebody in untold pain

and not helping them by getting rid of that pain for them. Let's help them die, I shouted vehemently in class in spite of the opposition.

The concept of Quality Adjusted Life Years (QALY) is a deeply rooted concept in medical law. QALY is a generic measure of the burden of disease on a patient, where the quality of life and the quantity of life is assessed. So a patients' year of life is adjusted for its quality. It is meant to help doctors determine how to go about certain conundrums for instance when there are two patients who both need an ICU bed.

Who should get the bed and for what reason?

In this case therefore, the quality of life say of a Stage 4 Cancer patient is measured if they are to be put in Intensive Care Unit. Will it be of help to them? Say if their life is to be put in comparison to that of a patient who just had an accident and also needs to be in the ICU. Who would the ICU add their quality of life? QALY is therefore largely against merely looking at the quantity of life of a patient. What value does their continued existence add?

I was supporting euthanasia all the way because I was of the opinion that the quantity of life did not matter much. I felt it was both a moral and legal right to let people go and not hold onto them for longer than it was necessary. Everybody deserves to die in dignity, I argued. Once somebody vegetated, it was already a slippery slope from there. Why not then allow them to have a dignified

death. What was this obsession of seeking to extend the length of life of somebody who was dying anyway?

I was being persuaded by several stories and offhand research that I had conducted over the internet and some library books. One of the stories was that of Brittany Maynard, who having Stage 4 Gliobastoma (Brain Cancer) had requested the right to die after being told she had a maximum of only six months to live. The state would not allow it, and yet Brittany felt her state of pain was also quite unbearable to her. She would end her life in her home from a lethal dose of barbiturates. That woman haunted me. That woman had merely just wanted to die in peace. That woman had merely wanted to die with her sanity intact. That woman had merely wanted to set her own terms.

What level of being inconsiderate was it that a woman had no control over her life? I asked the class while shouting at the top of my voice.

Just a few months earlier in June of that year, I had chanced upon the story of the great man that was Mr. John Shields, who when tormented by an incurable disease had said that he wanted dying openly and without fear to be his legacy. For him, his wish would come true. He would go on to even organize his own wake with music and alcohol and whatnot. Becoming debilitated and being tube-fed was something he held to be unacceptable to him.

"All those painful and demeaning things I considered beyond the threshold of how I would like to live. One quality of life that is important to me is my dignity- and sparing anxiety for my wife and daughter"

This case had been a positive case study for my course paper in Euthanasia. I thought John Shields interrogated the real meaning of dying a dignified man. It helped that just a year earlier the Canadian government had legalized the 'Medical Assistance in Dying' for competent adults who were suffering intolerably from irremediable diseases. So Canada had also provided great precedence for other countries. Several other countries had followed suit. I was actually suggesting that it was time for Kenya to consider accepting and incorporating assisted dying in our laws. The world was moving forward, not backward.

Nobody deserved to die in so much pain. I did not backtrack from this in any way all through to the end of the semester.

One of the most enduring questions to both the proponents and opponents of Euthanasia is whether "the right to a life with dignity includes the right to die with dignity".

In other words, the question was whether a dignified life should translate into a dignified death when one is encumbered by the rigors of a terminal illness for instance. And do they have a right to insist on dying with their dignity in place and to whom is this right enshrined. It's an open discussion to which at that level my answer was always a loud 'Yes'. I held that people should die with dignity; it was the least we would do to a person who was suffering untold pain.

A position I held until the day my father vegetated in his hospital bed. Until all his dignity had been stripped to shreds but it mattered not: all I cared about was only the fact that he was not dead.

Do everything you can to keep this man breathing.

His last morning, my father was breathing in scary shifts. Life was oozing out of him so thick, so fast and he would take so much time before he drew in any air. When I got to the hospital, I could see why my mother had said earlier that morning:

'This man will not make it past 8am".

His body was already growing stiff and his fingers were by this time damn ice cold. My mother was seated there with my aunt all waiting for the time the breathing would die away once and for all. He was making them wait. He was not dying already. And 8am was first closing in on us. My mother had particularly already given up and had not bothered to even clean him that morning because she had a premonition deep in her heart. It was going to be of no use if they were going to be handing him over to the mortuary as daylight approached.

That morning when his organs were now fast failing, the doctors would decide to fit him with an oxygen mask to assist in the breathing. One of the nurses whispered to me that it would add him only a few hours but his organs were already failing so fast he was a dying man no doubt because his kidney and liver were long gone. My aunts and to an extent my mum were furiously against the oxygen mask being fitted on him. They felt it was just a means of the hospital adding hospital expenses yet my father was already dead. They were discussing in hushed tones how some hospitals even kept dead people with Oxygen masks for close to a week.

They wanted the oxygen masks withdrawn so he could die in peace in 'God's appointed time'.

I was not hearing any of it. If that oxygen mask was going to add him fifteen goddamn minutes, then it was going to stay there. I wanted a little longer of daddy and I was ready to cause a ruckus about it. I needed my father even in his vegetative state. In whatever state as long as still breathing. They were going to keep that oxygen mask fitted on him for as long as he was still alive. Was it not me who had been cleaning his piss and shit? I could hear none of it.

An hour later, his doctor came to check on him and found a man so close to death I saw his heart skip a beat. Really, I did. He spent about five minutes checking his vitals and then called us to a different room. That's how

you know shit has hit the fan in the hospital. That's how you know the rubber has finally met the proverbial road. You somehow know the door is about to be shut when you are called to a different room.

"Austin, bring mum let's talk in the next room please".

"Mr. Omondi's organs have really been failing so fast. His kidney especially has had its functioning on a steep decline the last two days. As at this morning most of his organs have gone down so fast. With the state he is in, without stable breathing, Intensive Care Unit may not be of great help to him. It will not add any quality of life to him (Hear! Hear!) . The best thing to do is just have his family around him as he lives his last day".

He brought in the ICU specialist to explain the same thing to us.

I said they should take him to the ICU. Both the two doctors were against that idea.

I wanted to interject but my mum did so too.

"I am in total agreement with you Daktari. If very little can be done now then let's just be with him as a family. Let the Lord have His way"

Let the Lord have His way.

So I had to sit there as Dr. Okell had my mother sign consent documents that they were not to do anything anymore to Mr. Omondi. Basically, whatever the cause of death would be afterward, they were exonerating themselves.

Goddamit!

> "Your signing of this documents means that even if Mr. Omondi were to have a cardiac arrest this moment no doctor would rush in to resuscitate him"

That would be the moment I would realize euthanasia was nothing like we had romantically theorized it in the Medical Law class.

There was nothing like a dignified death.

This issue grossly transcended the person dying, to the people he was leaving behind.

If your brightest star was hooked to a hospital bed, dying: you clutched onto the last hours, minutes, seconds.

You fear for the gaping, irreversible hole he would leave if he stopped breathing.

I wanted my father alive, in any shape he came in.

I still do.

A few days before my father would pass away, my desperation would get peak high.

Two days before he actually passed on, I was growing

so irritated with how everything at Aga Khan Hospital was being run with a cavalier attitude. It was clear that the hospital were doing very little anymore to ensure Thomas came out of their hospital alive. They seemed to be mark-timing. I had long come to the conclusion that they were waiting for him to die to free up their bed space, so they would move on to the next patient. He was wasting their time still occupying that very expensive bed space that a better well-paying patient deserved more.

The nurses were especially growing awfully indolent in their duty, and the doctor was even more erratic in doing his rounds: there is in fact a day he never came at all. It was getting on my nerves. Nobody seemed to care anymore that there was a man in excruciating pain that needed not to die. They did not seem to care that there was a man in Ward 1 Bed 10 who depended on them for his life.

We have to transfer him to Nairobi and try another way out of this.

I had coordinated with my sister who was in Nairobi and we had been able to get a Red Cross Ambulance that had advanced life support machinations. I hoped we would transfer him that morning. It was going for Kshs. 65, 000 and I had no idea where I would get that kind of money and I assumed that even to others money was not as important as my dad's life. I remember telling the

lady at the Red Cross on phone that we would find the money as we travelled but before we got to Nairobi and she was insistent that payment had to be upfront.

"Young lady, my father is dying. Can you help me help him please? We will get all the money before we get to a hospital in Nairobi"

"I would love to Austine. But we can't flout the rules here. You can pay via any form, but the ambulance only leaves after payment. I am sorry."

"Let me consult and get back to you in a few"

I had hoped I would convince my mother to jump in on the ship to transfer him to a better facility in Nairobi.

My mother was already being such a pain. That morning she had told the nurse she 'was the only final decision maker in any matter concerning Mr. Omondi'. She was being such a hurdle. We were growing so irritated with each other she had told me she would slap me real bad, all this because I was questioning her every move.

I was questioning if she even wanted Daddy to survive in the first place because all she did was sit there and wait for the nurses and doctors to give two hoots and attend on my old man. Looking back, I know I was judging her quite harshly without considering the emotional roller-coaster she was probably facing on her end.

In retrospect though, I think she had already given up that early and I understand the hard stance she took on not moving him to any other place. Give it to her though; she had seen so many people in their death bed. She would tell me she had buried her three sisters three years in a row and that period had made her anticipate death from miles away. She knew when it was coming. She also seemed pretty sure death could not be treated, and there were no miracle workers in Nairobi who were going to do anything from what the doctors at Aga Khan were doing.

Let him die if that is what is meant to happen.

Let the Lord have his way.

That morning though, I was feeling we needed to try harder on Daddy. I recall getting back to the ward after the Red Cross call and telling my mum while crying that 'we can't be waiting for him to die like everybody else is already waiting. He is our father. We can't give up on Daddy. Let's put him in ambulance and even if he dies on it like Dr. Okell says, we can say we tried. Let's try harder. We can still save him. All we need to do is try. We've got to be able to say we tried our best with him"

My brother had been seated on the other side of the bed, forlorn, his face as hard as a cold cement floor. His eyes were blood shot, but he was hanging in there. Next to me, my mother was so withdrawn she was quietly seated, her mind not in the room. On the bed, my father

was shaking like a leaf being blown by wind, bordering on going manic. It seems like he had lost all his faculties already. He had been put for a fentanyl patch that had messed up with all his cognitive abilities. He just drooled continuously and shook his head in manic fits.

He would still not lie down on his bed due to the pain from both sides of his abdomen. He was really struggling to stay on float. He just sat on his bed: seeing nothing, saying nothing, shaking by a long chalk.

I broke into tears, long on desperation.

Then my mother motioned me and blurted;"What is wrong with you?"

"You don't cry in front of a patient. Go cry somewhere else"

So I quickly left the cubicle and went to wail in the washroom because I had gotten to the end of the tether. During the whole period my father was in hospital, this was actually the worst for me because I kept telling myself we had run out of time. I knew this was going to end miserably for us.

Three days later, we actually did run out of time.

Everything Suddening into a Hurricane

They say when someone dies; you miss the little things about them the most. You first miss those infinitesimal things about their lives that were every so often somewhat invisible. The little things about them that you may never have known you would hold close to your chest after their passing on. The little things about them that you most often always took for granted when they were alive. You miss the things you didn't realize even mattered at all: like how they would peel their banana from the middle in contrast to how everybody else would do theirs. It is only once they pass on that you realize how weird it is that they got rid of the entire banana peel before having the first bite.

You miss things that just lingered in the air waiting for you to realize they were significant. Instead of the more tangible attributes, you find yourself missing the most mundane of things: like how they had a wide gap between their teeth or how they clicked to show contempt whenever you made a dry joke. It is as if you become more alert after their passing on. I think we tend to ignore a lot of things when we imagine we have all the time in the world to experience them. We assume that there will be no disruptions to the world as we know it. Today, I am more present to the small things I encounter in my life than I was before I lost my dad and the fervent grandmother I was greatly fond of.

My father had a roaring laughter.

It was a thriving laughter.

It was loud and proud.

You couldn't miss it because it hit you at the right locus, and it most often came at the right time as it often came as a bolt from the blue. You could be discussing something so commonplace, and he would make a statement and burst out. He laughed with his whole body, too. He laughed like his laughter was the solution to all the problems that were bogging you down. You had him laugh and you imagined we had offset the entire Chinese debt that remains a millstone round our necks. Sometimes he would look at you as if he had not heard your joke and then out of the blue he just burst out laughing alone. I sometimes think he was not able to dial down on that laugh when it hit him like some sort of a high.

He could laugh, that man.

On the earlier days in his hospital bed, his body had really withered away but his laughter had not faded away at all. This was always so reassuring because most of those who visited him at that moment often felt he would be out of the hospital bed in no time. I remember he would tell most of them that he was already recovered; it's the doctors who were in fact wasting time instead of discharging him. He laughed with them as if the pain that was consuming his body was non-existent and yet at that very instant he was going through unimaginable and unbridled pain.

And so his guests would always certainly be comforted that he was dealing with such a minor thing: that cancer was not peeping from behind the curtains of his life mocking them as they thought the next day would be better. The next day never got any better. Neither did the next day after that. In fact, a train wreck was waiting to happen.

That is the problem with people that are larger than life.

Like my father, they could be dying but laughing their way through it and misleadingly soothing you in the process. There are so many things about my father that

I will greatly miss as evidenced by this book but I know for a fact that I will miss his laughter the most. So much, especially because I failed to soak it all in when he was alive. I failed to just sit still and experience the joy that was his laughter.

I hope he is keeping other people entertained with that laughter wherever that is.

I miss the spring in his feet. I miss how generous my father was whenever you needed his help. I miss his one liners that always contained so much wisdom. I miss how he just sat and listened for hours on end without any sort of compulsion to respond. I miss the fact that he was such a great teacher. I miss how he clicked when he wanted to show annoyance. I miss seeing his determination in practice. I miss every little thing about my old man. I miss the future we were supposed to share.

I miss his outstanding laughter.

I miss having a father to look up to.

On 10th June 2017, Juventus faced Real Madrid in the Champions League finals. It was a much waited for finals as Juventus had shown a real streak all through the championship and it also presented a break from the usual other finalists Barcelona and Bayern Munich facing with Real Madrid. Juventus were the underdogs who had been the better team all through the season. It needed no gainsaying that Real Madrid had cemented its place as one of the greatest teams in football this decade. One of its players, striking supremo Cristiano Ronaldo was on his way to winning his fifth ballon d'or and thereafter he would be buttressing his position as one of the all-time greats.

Most people I knew were rooting for a Juventus win. We all low-key always root for the underdog. We were all rooting for Gianluigi Buffon to hold a Champions League trophy as this was seemingly his final chance. He had had such a checkered career as a footballer (goalkeeper) and won so many championships. But the greatest trophy for any footballer had always slipped through his hands time and again. He had lost two Champions League finals prior to this finale and we had hoped he would lift it this time round. We were rooting for this underdog especially. We all sometimes feel that the small fry deserves a stab at success.

In less than 90 minutes, for a match that was extremely riveting, Juventus had been routed to a pulp. Four goals had effortlessly passed by the usually formidable shot stopper: the venerated Gianluigi Buffon who was a legendary goalkeeper even as we grew up. As the fourth goal by Marco Asensio fired past Buffon, the camera centered on him as he crawled on all fours trying to pick it up. It was done for them: for him. Cristiano Ronaldo had actually put two past him, and the clinical Casemiro had fired a volley from 30 yards. The match had turned

into a complete disaster for the Italian giants. They had been shredded to smithereens.

Jason Burt, writing for The Telegraph, would end his piece thus:

> "He has known defeat, known relegation, known the
> Calciopoli match-fixing scandal and a season in Serie B.
> He has also had battles in his private life, the darkness
> of depression having afflicted him. No one surely would
> begrudge him finally winning the European cup? But
> it did not happen. Sport can be romantic, lyrical, and
> sentimental even. But Buffon was denied his finale in the
> final. By the end, he was crashed'

Put plainly: It was heartbreaking that we had even held onto any sort of hope in the first place. Like it happened with certain flashing moments, I got myself greatly thinking about what loss meant even at that level despite it not being a life or death situation. I remember shooting a question to the table.

> "What do you think goes through the mind of a player
> after such a big time loss?"

> Chacha: "I don't know, man"

> Person X: "They are well counseled before such games.
> They surprisingly don't take football as personally as we
> do"

Me: "Look at Buffon man. Look at how these players are crying on this pitch. What do you mean they don't take such a loss personally?"

In football, the reality is there is almost always an either or outcome. Barring a draw on points, it's always just a win or a loss. And constantly, you are supposed to have it in your mind that there are days you will lose just as much as there are those you will emerge victorious. Some days it could be a polite lone goal, but other days you could be routed by a margin of even eight goals. And that's football: that's the nature of sports. I long learnt not to invest too much emotion into football, because you sort of learn that it cannot be that serious after all. I have however never got to accustom myself to the idea that loss can be a tolerable consequence of any event and that it should be taken in stride when it happens.

On that night though I got myself questioning what loss was actually supposed to feel like in the real world. In a world that was not football. Was it possible to have the right mind to lose and to know that it should be acceptable to lose sometimes? Could one get to a level where you were completely numbed to the pain of grief? Were there days you said this was not my day and actually accepted to live to fight another day? For a man like Buffon, who had lost three such finals, did it get to his heart anymore? Or was it the aforesaid case of 'We live to fight another day, for now we move on and regroup'. Did he actually think about it later that night or he just

tossed the thought aside as a bad day in the office? I, for sure, knew I would handle losing a Champions League final like a baby being taken off breast-feeding by the mother.

I think part of the reason it has taken me forever to get over the death of my father was because I had been so accustomed to winning in my life I could not handle a loss. I was raised content without any sort of suffering. I had overwhelmingly passed all my examinations right from primary School and now I was just waiting to graduate from Law School. I had been given everything by my father and I had not lacked anything I had wanted till then. I wasn't so welcoming of loss therefore at that moment. My life had been such a smooth sail. Before my grandfather died, I had not had such a great loss in our family. My maternal grandfather died in 1981 when my mother was still walking barefoot to school. There are a few other close family members that had died along the way but I had been too young to grasp the import of death. Everybody else thereafter was somehow always alive. My family seemed to have always been spared in the death business.

Then it hit me like a sledgehammer.

It is actually interesting how we seem to go through life thinking grief only belongs to other people. I had attended so many burials and for me it sort of was always a romantic experience as to how I felt sorry that death was dealing the bereaved the wrong hand. The Luo say that a funeral is quite sweet if it is at the neighbors. I never had the slightest clue that life always went full circle. I guess it is one of the very profound lessons I learnt when I lost my father. It could be me. Loss could actually be my portion too. I had seen families where death had swallowed up almost everybody and I had always concluded it is such people death harassed and that it was their fate in life. Fate is a foolish thing to take chances with.

I remember when my father died and I had to ask myself at some point almost concurrently,

"Why me?"

"Why not me?"

On the 10th of March 2017, my father had been slated to fly to Nairobi for further treatment at the Nairobi West Hospital. This was coming after my mother had shouted her voice hoarse to him that he was actually regressing badly until he had finally accepted to get further treatment. My dad had never wanted to be vulnerable at any given point, so he had adopted a don't-tell policy and all you saw was how reedy he had all of a sudden become. He told nobody nothing. When he was sick, he just stared at the ceiling and when you asked him he sometimes got really irritable about his condition. He was just there slowly relapsing into inaction.

A week earlier, my mother had insisted that I or Ian had to go take care of him because she had to go back to work and it was not advisable to leave him by himself. Being a high school Principal, and since she was teaching at a faraway location from our house, it was becoming difficult for her to always be there so she needed somebody to help her by being there with him and ensuring things were okay. I had been following up on some agendas of mine so after pestering Ian he had accepted to go. In retrospect, I think I should have gone home because I want to believe I could have pestered him to seek medical help earlier on. I think he would have done it out of wanting me to stop badgering him. That is therefore my guilt to live with.

Whenever you asked Daddy how he was doing, he always said he was okay. He did that to everybody. I remember the day my mother called me and told me 'don't say I didn't tell you' that I got so worried and called him. I told him Okay would not cut it this time round and he had to give me a percentage figure of how he was feeling.

'I'm 60% very fine. I will be 100% okay in no time.'

Three days earlier my mother had read to me his ultrasound report loudly as I wrote them down to consult. Immediately after the call, I would call Theodore to ask him what 'an enlarged liver' and 'minimal ascites' portended. He had nothing conclusive but gave me a

list of options we could consider. He mentioned nothing very serious so I knew it was not so bad after all. Looking back though, I remember how clearly he asked me who had those conditions and I replied my father and he said 'I'm sorry boss' but I hung up the phone so fast because its normal to say sorry if somebody is sick. It's only normal to say sorry, even if it were just a stomach upset.   Again, I should have prodded more. I should have listened to the tone in which he said sorry before hanging up. You stumble into a lot of 'I could have done' after losing someone thereby asking yourself 'Why didn't I?' These are those moments you spend the entirety of your life blaming yourself.

Every day after Ian travelled, I would call to find how the old man was doing. The conversation always went south.

'How is the old man doing?'

'This guy is bad'

'   Are you trying to be sensational like your mother?'

'Boss, you're not here. I am here with this guy every day.'

'But he is still driving. How bad can he be?'

'We shinda hapo'

I remember the day before he was to be airlifted to

Nairobi I asked him to give me a situation report using a rating of 1-10. '8/10'. That's truly the first time it hit me that this situation was taking a nose-dive for the worst. I had never even seen my father sick from a migraine and now those with him were saying he was actually dying. There was only so much sensation a person could spruce up. I especially knew he was very bad because my mother had said they had to take a flight that particular day.

My mother had told me that they would land at 11:45am so we were supposed to be picking them from the airport at 11am with an uncle of mine called Dan who works at Nairobi West Hospital. Dan had made arrangements so we would check him in in the private section of the hospital. By that evening as I left Nairobi West, we were just waiting for them to land the next morning and all preparations were in check. He would get the best treatment, Dan had assured me. I knew it was just a matter of time and Daddy would be back on his feet. Nothing bad was going to happen to him. Nothing bad could happen to him. He was the only shining armor in an extended family that largely depended on him. Surely God above must see that and see the need to spare his life.

"Please God let nothing bad happen to him"

That next morning when I woke up though, everything was amiss. I was up so early and tried to make myself breakfast and ran out of gas even before I could boil

bathing water. I therefore took a cold quick shower, walked the stretch from my house to the Kahawa Wendani stage and took the morning bus to town and then to Nairobi West Hospital and I remember being there by 9am. I was there before Dan himself, and he arrived a few minutes later and took me for breakfast at the hospital cafeteria and we were ready to proceed to hospital in a short while.

We would leave at 9:45am for the airport, to factor in that traffic gridlock that plagues Mombasa road on your way to the airport. Leaving hours early is just how you make it on time to anything in Nairobi though. Luckily, Dan had delayed a little longer at the office so at 10am we had not yet left the hospital. We were still in time though because my parents would be landing in about two hours earliest. I remember actually being in quite a rush that morning but everything was just not feeling right.

By 10am, my mum had called Dan that the flight would be delayed so we should not leave the hospital first. By 11am she was not picking my calls. At 12am, after waiting and calling so many times, she finally picked my call and told me there was a delay at the airport and they would not be traveling as scheduled and she would call to update me. She told me to just go back to the house. That was the first really red flag. Everything was suddening into a hurricane.

Everything had started going south.

I shot Ian a text.

"These guys are not travelling. I don't know why"

"There are two options here. Either they missed the flight or Mzee was declared too sick to get into a plane"

"Chief, I don't think somebody can get too sick to board a plane. I mean. It is only planes that carry incapacitated people"

"Aya. Wait and See"

At about 4pm, my mother finally called me that Daddy had been stopped from boarding at the airport. Reason? His legs were real swollen and they needed him to have a doctor certify that he could travel. They had not been able to score a doctor to do the same since he was also too weak, but they had got a doctor who was willing to run more tests and see what was up, so they were getting admission at Aga Khan Hospital Kisumu. The particular doctor had narrowed down the issue to the Liver. By this time I had panicked to the brim.

Fuck!

'I will leave first thing in the morning for Kisumu'

That night I was even more panicked. It still scores as one of the longest nights I have had. How sick must he

be that they could not allow him to get into a plane? I thought it was the illest of people who were carried in planes? I texted a buddy to ask him that and he would tell me: '…There is a difference between commercial planes and medical helicopters. What you see in movies are evacuation copters. Commercial planes have rules, and you need a certification from a doctor to travel when they consider you too sick. You don't want to be dying in a Kenya Airways and as a consequence occasioning a civil liability in their stead'

If not for the fact that I did not have a single clean attire to wear and carry, I would have travelled to Kisumu that same day. I had to quickly do my laundry that evening and I had told myself I would leave when they dried up, whatever time that would be. I was going to take care of my father. I had seen him take great care of his father and this was going to be my turn. The only difference is that nothing was going to happen this time round: nothing was going to happen to Daddy because he was my father.

They would not dry up until the next day 7am. Look how the universe conspires against us when we need it on our side most. I had checked them at 4am in the morning, and the trousers had been too wet to wear. Then I had routine checkups at 5am and 6am. It was only at 7am that I felt the trouser was wet but put-on-able. Still, it was quite wet. But wet meant nothing if my father was dying in a hospital in Kisumu. Wet was

manageable. I huddled a few of those clothes in my bag and left for Kisumu.

The previous night, unable to sleep at all, I texted my girlfriend:

"My father is really sick and has been admitted in Kisumu and I am going there tomorrow to be with him. I do not know what will happen to him, but I hope nothing bad happens because I am not done having a father."

On that day as I travelled to Kisumu, I was such a disturbed man. I was so confused and agitated. I was really troubled. The car I had boarded in town was greatly delaying, and my elder sister who had left home a bit later was already Kisumu bound in a shuttle. I bought myself a hotdog in Tuskys to calm me down (I like chewing when angry) and then threw it into a City Council dustbin. My chest was heavy, my hands sweaty and I had a splitting headache that was making my eyes so dense. I was a ball of despondency and raw fear.

While on the journey, I remember the most pressing question to me was:

'Maaaaaaaan, what can we do without Daddy if he were to die?'

It was such a scary question, but it is on that journey that it was prominently occurring to me that my father could actually be dying. I had not even seen him for three months and my mind was already wandering that much. It is not something you want to think about, but you think about it anyway. It clouds your mind, and consumes you. You cannot avoid it. In such moments, mortality flashes right before your eyes. You lose balance. We are all mortals.

Again, I had not seen him. I did not know what his condition was, and yet I was really worried. The last time I had left him at home in January, he was a fine man, just slightly losing his health. Apart from the incessant stomach aches, he complained about nothing else. He had his balance and he ate perfectly well. Now I had no idea how he even looked but the fact that he had been chased from the airport sunk my heart down the gutter. I had to do something and yet the truth was that there was only so much I was able to do.

"How sick must one be to be chased from the airport surely?"

And well, when I got to Kisumu, I was accosted by a reedy man unlike the man I had left home. I remember I found so many people huddled at the lounge waiting to see him and my mum quickly pointed me to where he was. He was so pale with sunken eyes: yellow sunken eyes. He had lost so much weight the bones on his neck were protruding. His teeth were yellow, his laughter not reassuring. Even his voice was greatly muffled. He spoke one word at a time. He was exhausted and he was clearly in pain. He was a complete disaster. And yet he looked at me and smiled, as if happy to see me.

'I should have listened to my mother."

They were seated with Emily at the CT Scan lobby and I remember them joking at how dumbfounded I was:

"Don't look at a sick person like that. You can 'add' him sicknesses" he said and smiled amusingly.

Then he burst into his signature laughter.

———————————————

All the ultrasound results ever showed was that Daddy had an enlarged liver or a liver enlargement or enlargements in the liver, everybody we sort advice from put it differently. The lab technician told me it was not obvious from the ultrasound reports what the swellings were and so their cause would not be known. So the doctor, Dr. Ogutu, merely looked at it and prescribed drugs as he did on the other occasions. He gave it no more thought than that. So my father, in good shape, went back home with his enlarged liver. His legs were already swollen then, a condition known as edema. So here was a man with a swollen liver and swollen legs walking around like nothing was going on. And my grandmother told me he was doing a pretty good job hiding the swollen legs. He was not leaving the insides of the car when he went to see her. He said Hi through the car windows and left almost immediately.

My mother was getting so worried, as my father deflected everybody that he was doing just fine. She was applying so much pressure on him from all angles, and he was still working so hard to ignore him. But when she persisted, it is from this pressure that he would accept to fly to Nairobi for treatment because by then he had tried Aga Khan Kisumu enough times. He had been getting worse, and he was beginning to suspect Dr. Ogutu was merely siphoning money from him with reckless abandon. His cousin Dan had assured him he would be there to ensure he got top of the range services at Nairobi West Hospital, and so he had agreed to that. He was coming to Nairobi to get back on his feet.

"I have suffered enough" he would tell me in his hospital bed when I asked him why he had waited for his condition to get that bad. He had come to accept he was not as fine as he was telling everybody. By that time though, it was apparent that it was too little too late.

That's how my father, on the 10th March, ended at the airport, got chased over his edema and on 11th March ended back again at Aga Khan Kisumu to begin a new battery of tests. This time, the doctor had changed to Dr. Julius Okell, the resident nephrologist at the hospital. He sounded assuring. He sounded like a gentleman who had an idea of what he was doing. And after Dr. Ogutu, we needed a doctor who sounded like he knew what he was doing. He touched his stomach just once and told them 'this is not a stomach problem, this is the liver, and

there is something wrong with your liver'. He sounded like the doctor who was going to help him out of the excruciating pain he had endured, and so my father gave him a chance with his life. A chance to give him another stab at a healthy life.

He (Dr. Okell) thus wanted to be sure what the problem was so he could then advise on what step to take. He was however quite positive it was a Liver condition. By then, my father had done the test for Hepatitis (negative) and Liver cirrhosis (negative). Those two were the common illnesses that affected the Liver. Those were the two easy ways out. Other than those two, it was a slippery slope. It was downhill, but still the doctor, like all doctors, was trying to reassure us that he didn't think it was anything major. In my mind, the moment the Hepatitis and Liver Cirrhosis were ruled out I told myself it was going to be the worst prognosis for Daddy. I could only think of Cancer.

The first thing he advised was for a CT scan to be done.

A computerized tomography (CT) or computerized axial tomography (CAT) scan combines data from several X-rays to produce a detailed image of structures inside the body. A CT scanner emits a series of narrow beams through the human body as it moves through an arc. This is different from an X-ray machine, which sends just one radiation beam. The CT scan produces a more detailed final picture than an X-ray image. The CT scanner's X-ray detector can see hundreds of different levels of density. It can see tissues within a solid organ. This data is transmitted to a computer, which builds up a 3-D cross-sectional picture of the part of the body and displays it on the screen.

The preparatory procedure for the CT scan was quite a challenge for Daddy. There is a certain solution you are required to take for two hours that contains certain medical drugs that are supposed to clear your system pre-procedure. The problem is the solution can induce vomiting, which is not required since the solution is needed in your body. He was easy to vomit, and he could vomit even without eating. He managed to drink without vomiting and when I asked him he said he had been drinking it 'mathematically like the mathematician he was". It was clear though that he had gone through hell drinking that concoction.

When the CT scan report came the next day, it showed that there were several injuries to his liver that had caused it to enlarge. From the scan images, you could see there were several white spots on his liver. In the report, the radiologist had opined in a 'sub-report' that this was characteristic of 'Hepatic Metastases'. Hepatic Fucking Metastases. Hepatic Metastases refers to a cancerous tumor that has spread to the liver from a cancer that started in another place in the body. It's also called secondary liver cancer or Liver metastases. Everything was suddening into a hurricane.

The Hepatic metastases issue was in the sub-report, and not the main report. I remember my mother constantly asking me to Google for her what that was, and I was deflecting. I knew all she would see would be the word Cancer. It would kill her, considering we had really been praying that it would be anything else but not cancer. We were holding our fingers that Daddy did not have Cancer. I was reciting it to myself all the time: Daddy does not have Cancer. He cannot have Cancer.

Lord, let this be anything but not the deadly Cancer. It already took away Mzee just five months ago. It cannot strike us twice. Let it not Good Lord.

So it was a relief when the doctor came in the next day and did not pronounce Cancer on us. He said the test was not conclusive at all. If indeed it was the metastases, then they needed to find out where it was coming from, Where the Cancerous cells were spreading from. He therefore ordered for an endoscopy and a colonoscopy to act as follow up tests to help develop a better prognosis. He therefore temporarily handed over that to the resident endoscopist, Dr. Susan Kaittany.

The procedure for endoscopy and colonoscopy is not fancy needlework either. There is another preparation liquid that you are supposed to take in order to clear your system. For 24 hours, that is all that is allowed to get into your system. No solid food or thick liquids. I remember after my father had done his preparation for over 24 hours and the nurses were beginning to say they were not sure if the doctor was coming in for the procedure, he got so angry the nurses had to get hold of Dr. Kaittany. You do not starve somebody for 24 hours and casually postpone the procedure, he argued. We got hold of the doctor.

By 12am that morning, we were wheeling him down to the theatre for the procedures. He was emaciated, weak and dejected. The attendant nurse was trying to cheer him up with the prospect of food after the procedure and he just vacuously stared at her. He called me back to his ward to ask the nurses to get him some food. The procedure had been successful, but the doctors had used little anesthesia and so he had woken up in the middle of the procedure and seen the rest of it, as uncomfortable as that had been for him. I cursed at the incompetence. Later in the evening, he told us with mum that Dr. Kaittany had told him that there was nothing major from the two procedures. She was going to analyze the pictures, but he was not supposed to be worried. I remember he slept for more than an hour that night, albeit on his plastic seat. That was a little re-assuring.

There was nothing major.

That would become our rallying cry for the next week before Daddy passed on.

Even when the results of the two procedures delayed the next day, we sat easy because there was nothing

major. And when the results came back, everything was neat and pretty, apart from a case of severe gastritis in the stomach. I quickly googled that and realized it was merely a severe case of ulcers.

Ah, we were good.

There was nothing major.

This cancer thing that was rearing its head in the name of hepatic metastases was merely a scare. I asked the doctor if we were supposed to be worried about it, and she schooled me on the meaning of "indicative", because those CT Scan Results had merely been an indication and not a conclusion in itself. So, again, there really wasn't anything to be worried about.

There was nothing major.

The next day however, the same doctor ordered for a biopsy, which was the final test that could be done to diagnose cancer. From all the procedures already done, they had not been able to come up with any diagnosis, and so they wanted Daddy to do a biopsy to be able to conclusively give a Cancer diagnosis. At this time, the only conclusion was going to be what type of cancer it was. If this was not conclusive, then it was going to be witchcraft and we were going to have to look for people who healed witchcraft.

Everything was suddening into a hurricane.

In my entire life, before my grandfather and father passed on, the only other two people who had died and were close to me were Marvin and NyaPwoyo. They had both passed on when I was still a young boy and the veracity of what the death of a close person portended was still lost on me. My best friend, Marvin, would die when I was only eight years old and Nya Pwoyo, my other mother, would die before I joined high school. I never even got around to knowing her government names. My mother would tell me about her death months after it had happened, in her usual light banters. I felt a sharp sting of pain when she told me about her last days with cervical cancer but I cannot say I lacked sleep because of it.

As a child growing up in the winding and dusty roads of Rang'ala, Master Marvin Ooko and I were the best of friends. Until today, he is the only memory I have of a best friend: the one semblance I have had of a best friend in my entire childhood. I have extremely great friends even today, ones who have stood by me through thick and thin, but none of them closes in on Marvin. It could be because we were very young then, but whenever I look back at those days, I was a full human being. Whenever I was at their home, it would take threats from my mother to get me back to our place. She would send the maid to deliver threats of endless whooping if I did not go back home immediately. And the same would happen

with him, but her mother was always the laid back one. Sometimes, it would take a beating for us to be separated. We were as mischievous as they come, and sometimes we would steal money from our parents to achieve a mischievous end. I always wound up in serious beating, and being the last born, he would always be let off with a warning. So he always did more of the stealing. I know I loved him to bits.

Marvin was an extremely creative fellow. He was good with his hands, making a motley of creative paraphernalia with them: cars, lorries, houses, people, and airplanes. He would use a simple mound of clay to build the Sunblest lorry that always passed by the roadside every day early in the morning delivering bread to the local retailers. At any given point, he was always creating something. He was a hands-on fellow, that Marvin. We used 'Master' before our names because even at that level, we always wanted to be unique from the rest. We were two young and yet too elitist. It did not help that the best position in class was always a competition between the two of us. He always beat me, but I always lived to fight the subsequent term, drowning in those primary two books as he laughed at my vanity. I beat him on countable occasions. In our elitist bubble therefore, we interacted with nobody else. He was my only friend as I was his. With the benefit of hindsight, it was a pinch of hubris that we lived with.We were cool cats.

It destroyed me when his mother, a secondary school

teacher, was then transferred to Sinaga Girls High School and they had to move. It took me days to come to terms with that fact, as I was losing the only friend I had since we joined Nursery School. But some of these things you have no control over as a seven year old kid, so you suck it up. A year later we began communicating through letters that would be delivered by our mothers. He informed me he was doing well and he was intending to join a boarding school, Gulf Academy and that I was supposed to join it too. So I convinced my mother and she said I would be joining the school as I joined Standard 5. We were in constant communication despite the fact that we never saw each other that year but our mothers would constantly meet.

Then one bright Saturday morning my mother told me Marvin had been run over by a Pick Up from behind and he had died on the spot. It had happened on the Thursday of 6th September 2001. Just like that. A pick-up had delivered some goods at their place, and as it left, he jumped onto it in that way cheeky kids do, and it ended badly. My best friend was gone. Until very many years later, I was unable to process the death of Marvin: my class prefect, my competitor, my best friend. We buried him on 15th September 2001 and I remember attending and feeling great remorse but not grief. Years later, it affected me that Marvin was not there to celebrate even in my smallest of achievements. I miss him, still. I miss the prospect of what he would have been today: of what we would have been today. I think about Marvin a lot these days as I miss my father. He was an awesome human being.

Nya Pwoyo was always like our other mother. She made us food during lunch hours as our parents slaved off in the classrooms teaching. She loved us so much, I bet like she did her own children. I know she treated me like her own child and she loved me to a fault. We were staying at Ugunja with my mother and my father was still staying at Rang'ala boys where he was the Principal. We were studying at Rang'ala Boys Primary then. So Nya Pwoyo would make some break time tea as we sneaked back home and would make us lunch. She made delicious eggs. She loved making them in a certain way and it's what we ate most of the times. I was extremely fond of her because she was always so wise, and she was always laughing revealing her removed lower teeth bank area, as per the Luo Customs of her time yet she was actually Luhya.

As my father got transferred and we moved homes, we lost contact because by then I had joined boarding school. We had also moved permanently to Ugunja and I never for once made the trip to visit her. Then one day my mother told me she had died, of Cervical Cancer no less and that her last days had been so painful. A death she never deserved: the same thing I would think about as my father lay on his hospital bed writhing in excruciating pain. She had no money and so cancer had eaten her up to death at her home. I found it very sad and I think it was the first time I had somebody I know die but only know about it several months later. It is only several years later that I got around to visiting her home and seeing her grave and breaking down. Rest Easy Mama Okello.

Grief is such a complicated thing. It is not as linear as people expect it to be. People believe grief should be a four stages thing. That you should allow yourself to go through the four stages of grief and then emerge healed on the other end. You are not allowed to deeply grieve, or the society will think you need some sort of divine help. You are allowed to be deeply into other mundane things such as football or TV series like Game of Thrones but you cannot be the guy who deeply grieves, because you need to 'move on'. You must move on. The various stages of grief are therefore constantly recited to you as if in an opera: Denial, Anger, Bargaining, and Acceptance.

But grief is not an order thing. You do not go through an order while grieving, most people actually don't. I didn't feel like I was going through any order as I went through my grief. Some days, I was in deep denial that my father was dead: I was constantly trying to drum into my brain that he was going to walk through the door and tell me to vacate his seat as he always did. On the same day, when he didn't walk in through the door, I

accepted he was gone: that he was never coming back at all. It was a mixed feeling of experiences. There are days I bargained with myself that it had been the wrong time for my father to die, and yet he was in so much pain in his hospital bed that he had needed to die urgently. On those days, I was always quite angry. I always felt in one way or another I had myself to blame for his death.

The one thing I however walked with in my journey of grief was depression. I was constantly disturbed. I cried myself to sleep on most nights like a jilted woman. My father's death had made me, in the words of Cheryl Strayed, feel that I could not continue to live. I was feeling extremely worthless in the days that followed the burial and I spent most of the time in the village with my mother who I suspect was going through the same thing. That death had broken me, and I was not going to pretend it was not killing me. Sometimes I tried to share my depression with my friends, but they almost always didn't know what to do. We do not know how to handle grief, understandably so. I am the leader of the tribe, and it was difficult opening up most of the times. So I sucked it up and dealt with it.

Grief is everything suddening into a hurricane.

The Crack of Dawn

You will know at the crack of dawn. You know so because almost every survivor says they knew at the crack of dawn. You also know so because you knew at the crack of dawn. You woke up suddenly at five in the morning and knew right away that the day had come. You were not scheduled to do anything that day and yet there was no more sleep forthcoming. Your mind seems set and you annoyingly wonder why it had to choose a Monday of all the dumb days. Mondays are supposed to portend a fresh start. The truth is that you had hoped for a Saturday. It is quite startling to you how a chilly Monday morning can herald the beginning of the end. You make a mental note of the things you need to take care of first and realize you've got to get running. First, you go outside and smell the fresh morning air and feel the cold breeze hit your face. It rained the previous night so there is also the refreshing smell and allure of wet soil.

It is such a beautiful day to give up.

You go back into the house and settle down to write the note.

Human beings are in a constant state of motion. You wonder how it is that to live is to be in motion. Your friends have moved on to new careers and relationships and countries and are literally living their best lives while your life seems stuck in a rut. Everybody seems to have a reason to wake up in the morning. You wake up in the morning and ask yourself for what is it worth.

This guy you didn't know in the estate has been found dead in his house. It is your Boda guy that calls to give you the deets and you rush there to see for yourself. He hanged himself at six in the morning. You marvel at his bravery as every other person at the scene marvels at his cowardice. You almost take that as your sign but the thought doesn't linger for long in your mind. You know you will know at the crack of dawn. There is a short conversation amongst the onlookers about suicide as an option and this burly guy says people who commit suicide should be thoroughly flogged first and then given a no casket burial to serve as a lesson. For a brief moment people at the scene consider it.

To live is to make a choice. For a long time, you never understand that to die can be to make a choice too. You have lived your life pretty well-guarded from all the vagaries of life. A happy family. Parents that were always your last line of defence. Healthy friendships. Gone to great schools. Always in amazing relationships. You are a fat happy child. You wonder what would make anybody decide to kill themselves. One time you tell a friend who says they are depressed that they have become a woman. You say it in jest but that friend never comes back to you for help. Your mind is such a minefield of joy and stability that you imagine that is the constant of life. Only several years later do you realize that a stable mind is the greatest blessing a human being can hold. The majority of people are walking traumas.

It is the death of your father that first shakes your world to the highest Richter scale. You are a young boy barely out of University. Your father is your true North. In point of fact, he is your entire compass direction. After his passing on, you wonder how you should move on with your life directionless. It is the very first time you tell yourself you cannot continue to live anymore. For what is it worth? Don't we all live to make someone else proud of us? For you that person is your father. He dies as you hold his hands and you wonder how cruel even God can be. You try to maintain a brave face as the world beneath your feet crumbles. You are completely gutted. You assure yourself that you only need to live a day at a time because it does get better. It doesn't get better.

It is not the death of your father that breaks your back though. It is the permanence of grief. It is the spiraling effect of everything you lose after losing your father. You

lose your best friend Brian when all he has done is stick in your corner. This happens because you continually project your frustrations to him and he expectedly gets fed up putting up with your shit. You lose a beautiful relationship that was really blossoming because you feel needlessly unworthy. You lose interest in school and barely attend classes. You lose work. You lose interest in a career that you have worked hard to get to since you were five, never even once changing your mind. You lose sleep every day. You lose family because grief is such an intense personal journey for everyone. You lose yourself.

The decision to end the pain is an agonizing choice. You make the decision but have to wait for the right time. The crack of dawn. You walk around knowing your days are numbered without knowing with any exact precision. You go to class and visit friends and go for drinks and have sex yet the prospect of continued living is not appealing to you anymore. You are always making preparations of how to bow out. You read several articles and scour You Tube searches for the most painless way to do it. When you find it, you wait for the right moment with everything precisely planned. You wait for the crack of dawn.

You file away the note neatly in the coat pocket you intend to put on.

You go back outside and it is mid-morning and everybody

seems to be in a hurry. You know that once you exit, life will continue like this. People will continue with their shit unnerved by your exit. You think about your closest friend who now has a bundle of joy. That little girl gives him so much life you know he will be fine. You think about your friends who will enjoy the road trip to Masiro. You know they will wonder how you call yourself a Luo when your village is full of Luhyia people. You think about family and know they will do just fine. You doubt there is anything in the world that your mother cannot come out of. She has always managed to rise from any rock-bottom situation. You however make an interesting decision at this point. You decide to call her. You imagine you want to listen to her voice if only one last time.

It is the tremor in her voice that jolts you back from your reverie.

You have never looked back at that day as the day you escaped death by a whisker. You merely think of it as the day you made the decision to live a little longer for your sick mother. You pack up and go spend time with her believing it would be your last deed of kindness. You thereafter decide to feel a little more. To try a little better. The thing about getting back on your feet is that you know it will take you the longest time. But you are willing to work through the fog of grief. You want to see what more life can probably have to offer. You want to commit to forever take care of your mother. You hope there will be no other consequential crack of

dawn in the near future. You go for therapy. You write an apology to your best friend that goes unanswered. You move in with your brother for company. You go back to postgraduate school. You start looking for work. You make new friends. You take a shot at a new lease of life.

A few months into your new lease of life, you lose your doting grandmother: a woman you constantly fawned over and who loved you to a fault.

And the epicenter of your life is shaken once more.

And you begin to wait for the crack of dawn once again.

Cusp of Misery

The first Tuesday after we buried my grandfather, I would be sandwiched in between two commuter buses in the Nairobi Central Business District. It had happened in a split second. I was headed back to Campus from running an errand in town for my mum. It had been an easy evening. I had met my good friend Ricky Thomas for cold beers and as we parted ways, I had used the wrong alleyway to the bus station at the Koja roundabout. It was a basket case of being at the wrong place at the wrong time doing the wrong thing.

I had only noticed I was sandwiched when the metallic rails in one the buses firmly gripped onto my thighs and I was feeling a searing sensation on the edges that held the rails. Yet the driver was still reversing against the front of the bus on the back. It is like he was either not using the side mirror or he was bound to hit the other bus without the intention to. Or he was just being the archetypal Nairobi matatu motorist who threw any caution to the winds.

I could hear women shouting to the driver of that particular bus that was reversing, about to press me into a neat sandwich. Those two buses were going to squeeze me into nothing but a mass of tempered meat and blood. I had heard stories of how this had happened to a couple of people who had been pressed in between two buses in the CBD. I had actually seen a TV feature story of this girl who had been pressed by two buses just near the same spot I was facing this predicament.

This was my proverbial brush with death.

You can wake up on a beautiful sunny Monday morning and do everything right only to make one wrong move and you could find yourself sandwiched in between two buses in the Nairobi CBD. Fate decides if you wake up in the morning, and if by sheer luck you do, going back to bed at night could be the elusive part. Such is our journey of life. That even an extremely good day can take a turn for the worst in an instant. We walk around with our fates in the palm of our hands and yet not knowing what it portends. We live our lives unaware of how it is the split second decisions that determine our destinies.

Paulo Coelho says of fate:

"I can control my destiny, but not my fate. Destiny means

there are opportunities to turn right or left, but fate is
a one-way street. I believe we all have the choice as to
whether we fulfill our destiny, but our fate is sealed"

We dance with destiny. We choose what we do with
the time we have. Our lives are a constant attempt to
chase shadows, to make sense of what we are meant to
be. We can have control of at least some of the things
that happen to us but there are those things we come to
realize are beyond us. One of the most beautiful sayings
I have learnt to live by is by Elizabeth Gilbert when she
says:

> "There is so much about my fate that I cannot control,
> but other things do fall under the jurisdiction. I can decide
> how I spend my time, whom I interact with, whom I share
> my body and life and money and energy with. I can select
> what I can read and eat and study. I can choose how I'm
> going to regard unfortunate circumstances in my life-
> whether I will see them as curses or opportunities. I can
> choose my words and the tone of voice in which I speak
> to others. And most of all, I can choose my thoughts."

On that day as I had this astonishing cold brush with
death, I remember asking myself as I slipped into a trance,
could this be it? Is this how it ends for me? Sandwiched
in between two buses? Is it my fate to die like the child
of a lesser God? Who even dies pressed in between two
buses? Fuck it, am I about to die in a worse way than
my grandfather just did a week ago? Somebody help me

please. I tried to shout at that moment and what came out was some muffled sound. This is it.

What the fuck is this happening to me now and I have a date with my campus crush this evening in my room that I took a month to arrange? I remember thinking that too in that confusion.

I pissed in my trouser. I always remember it very clearly because it came out as if I was in the washroom and not in panic droplets. It was not that piss that sneaked out, it was a very deliberate one. Then everything else after that pissing session became an abstraction. I think I may have soiled myself more.

When I came back from the reverie, I was lying on the tarmac facing up, my thighs too heavy and my legs unable to move. I tried to stand up and it seemed like a tall order so I just lay there for a few minutes. Luckily, nothing major had happened to me. Those women had saved my life. They were shouting to the driver to find a way of taking me to hospital before I died. Then I was being rushed to a medical facility. It was such a scare I told nobody anything about it even later on that evening, only giving a few details to my then Campus roommate Peter Onunga, a fine gentleman by all means, who would later on insist on escorting me for more tests with my campus inamorata to the University Health Centre. Surprisingly, there wasn't any major injury, and I had escaped with just a few blisters on the upper part of my thighs that had been held by the metallic rails.

I owe my life and even just my ability to write this book today partly to those women who began wailing in time, the women who sell all manner of goods by the side of the street and I would pass them in a hurry to do my other important things. The women we all pass like they mean nothing, yet here three of them saved my life. I do not know them, but I always hope fate rewards them. I think about them, still, a lot. I am today very cautious of how I treat people who do all sorts of menial jobs because I know some day it could be my life on their hands again. That experience opened my eyes to why we all matter in the grand scheme of things.

That would be my second major brush with death only second to the moment I drowned at the Kenyatta University swimming pool in January 2013, a traumatic experience that has kept me on the shallow end of swimming pools since then. I had gone swimming with my best friends Theodore and Brian and they had assumed I was a pro. I saw them diving on the deep end and I followed in tow believing that swimming was not some fancy needlework. I almost died on that day because they did not realize I had been drowning until it was quite late. Today, if I have to swim I scramble for that shallow space with kids all the time. Recently though, I can do half the swimming pool. We are making progress on that front.

For the whole of the week that followed that traumatic bus experience, death stalked me like a bitch. It harangued me in my dreams. I was seeing every close person to me facing their death in one manner or the other. What if somebody got into our house and hacked my father to death now that he was living alone? What if my mum got involved in a motorbike accident, now that she rides in them all the time? What if Ian choked on alcohol now that he drank too much? How about Emily stopped going to Eastleigh because it was a terrorist den? I felt a whisper of death all around me.

I especially thought about cancer all the time. It was now in the family. It was coming for my father. It was coming for me. Even the doctors - in my nightmares - were calling it a rare type of cancer. The cancer that had eaten up Mzee was beginning to get into my head, and I was slowly losing myself thinking it was going to end badly for my dad and even myself. I had read a little bit about cancer, and my paranoia was on extreme levels, an all-time high. Death stalked me like a young suitor does a beautiful woman: deliberately.

Man, I thought a lot about Cancer those days. I think a lot about cancer even today. It follows me. I am today very aware of what cancer is and how much it takes away. I am today very particular of what should happen to me should I get cancer. I saw what it did with my father and the rehearsal before that on my grandfather. I know fate has its own plans with my life, but I am very aware of how I want my end to look like should I be diagnosed with cancer. I have had an opportunity to interrogate that possibility as I discuss elsewhere in this book.

When my father told me he was having stomach issues in January, I frequently asked him to go for a colonoscopy and an endoscopy. I was reading from the script of a book I had read where the writers' husband had ended up with a colon cancer diagnosis from mere stomach infractions. I even told my mother and uncle at some point to ask him to consider those two tests. Carla Malden had contended that she believed her husband would have been saved if they had gone for the colonoscopy even just a month earlier. I insisted my father go for the tests and they were not reading from that script.

On the day he was admitted, I remember having an argument with my mother about liver cancer, because the doctor had ruled out all other major liver diseases. I sort of knew he would go down with cancer. When I landed in Kisumu and saw the frail man that was waiting for a CT scan at the Aga Khan lobby, I remember thinking to myself: 'Here we go! Let this not be a cancer', a feeling I would maintain throughout our ten day period at the hospital until the day the doctor would casually tell us he thought what was ailing Thomas was hepatocellular carcinoma. I would know it was cancer even before Googling whatever the hell that was.

In the dead of the night on my bad days, I dream I will go down with cancer too. And so be it. As I write this, a Kenyan entertainment leading light has just recently died of brain cancer, and it is such a gut-wrenching feel for me, despite not knowing him personally. Big Kev was a towering godfather to the entertainment scene in Kenya, and yet Cancer put him down, ate him piecemeal and then chewed him out. Several more celebrities and public figures have bowed out due to Cancer this year and many more are battling the disease. The indefatigable John McCain has bowed out and we lost Janet Ikua Kanini too. The indomitable Safaricom CEO has just passed on due to acute leukemia at 60 and he was followed by Ken Okoth the former Kibra parliamentarian who was followed by Dr. Joyce Laboso the former Bomet Governor. It is a mess out here. There is a cancer epidemic in this country. Professor Makau Mutua even argues that cancer is the new AIDS in Kenya.

There is cancer all over the place in Kenya. You bump into it being discussed in television segments, being written about in newspapers or even just being bantered about in ordinary settings. Everybody knows someone who has battled cancer. It could be a mother, sister, brother, uncle, cousin, father, grandfather. There is always someone.

Until this day, my mother says I may have foretold my fathers' cancer because I used to ask her about the genetics of Cancer all the time. I researched on

the percentages and the probabilities a lot. After my grandfather died of cancer, I knew that somebody was next at home, because 'cancer was now in the family'. The problem is I always thought that next person was going to be my father. Every time I talked about it with my mother, she would tell me my father has over 8 siblings, why I thought it was my father or myself who would be affected by the genetics of it was downright paranoia. This was until it was not downright paranoia.

Until it really wasn't downright paranoia.

The same incident would be replicated after the death of my father when I would ask Dr. Okell about what my probability of suffering the same fate was. All he did tell me was not to worry about things I had no control over and that numbers and figures were just that: numbers and figures. I saw my mother and uncle shrug when I asked this question. But the good doctor eventually did mention a 5% chance.

I hope and pray I don't ever have to worry about numbers and figures for my children. I hope they stay as just that, numbers and figures.

The Sunday of that week that I would have my brush with death at the Koja Bus Station, unable to sleep past eight in the morning, I would attend the Sunday Christian Union service at my campus. My mind greatly hazy, I would sit through the whole service: a first for the whole of that year. By that time, I had gotten to the

questioning face of religion where I thought Christianity did not even matter in the first place.

A young beautiful lady would coincidentally preach on - 'how to counter evil thoughts". Her Solution: "Rebuke the thoughts in the name of Jesus". I don't know how that would work in real life, but I assume that it would for those who have great faith already. Those who spend their day dreaming and thinking of the milk and honey in heaven and who have trained their thought process not to veer into the worldly order of things. I was not that guy. I am not that guy. I was a guy constantly thinking about his own death and what would happen if the world swallowed me. I know today that that period was one of the worst periods I have had to live through.

A week later, I would start my final campus exams and the nightmares would lessen.

Small bits of dreams still harangued me in my sleep sometimes informing me that my father was gravely ill or that he was dying or that he was in some form of trouble I could not place my hands on during the nightmares. What I didn't know was that I was foreboding what would happen because right in the middle of my final semester law examinations that year, my mother would call me that my father was extremely indisposed at home and wanted me to go back home before the holidays began.

She said he had acute ulcers: he said he had severe

abdominal pains.

I made a mental note that I would be seeing them in ten days as I travelled to the country side for the Christmas holidays. I always spent my Christmas holidays in the village to run away from the hustle and bustle of Nairobi. It was constantly occurring to me that I had never known my dad to be vulnerable or even sick that would make my mother call in distress, and this was going to go down to the wire. The rubber had met the legendary tarmac and my dreams were nolonger just dreams.

Two months after burying his own father, my father would begin to die.

———————————————————

"Omera even the worst of days have to be lived; you cannot give up in this life until the last moment comes", my father told me in his hospital bed in our conversations on the early days when he had just been admitted. He could not eat, drink nor sleep and it did not bother him because those were just bad days and they were clearly just a passing cloud. He saw those days as nothing more than a bad day at the office. Most of the times, it is actually me who felt most of his pain. He seemed to have numbed to it.

On the evening of March 22nd, I remember how I had been having stuttered breathing the whole day and I had not slept a wink the previous night. There was a heavy

clog in my chest that seemed to be hindering my draw in of air. At some point, I was fast losing breath. I could not breathe in normal fashion; it was like I was holding my breath without my will because what came out sounded like a cats purr. I had been feeling extremely awful the whole day my heart was beginning to sink too. There was a stinging pain that was coming from the left side of my chest and I knew it was not something I would attribute to loss of sleep. What was happening to me?

The previous day, I had not slept for the reason that Daddy had had such a difficult night he had not been able to sleep a wink and was in a great deal of pain. He just tossed and turned on the seat he had positioned himself in, his eyes fully awake and his pain unbearable. The edema (swelling) in his legs had now increased so I rested his legs on my thighs so that they were not hanging from the bed. He wasn't able to lie on the bed because there was a stinging sensation from both sides of his stomach, caused by the severe damage that had happened to the liver. So he just sat there in this rickety plastic chairs and tried to get some sleep, which mostly did not happen.

That was a really agonizing moment for me, and I bet him too.

By that evening, it was becoming pretty clear that his time was seemingly beginning to run out real fast. Rather, the palliative care doctor had told us without any remorse that we were supposed to be counting his hours and not days anymore. With feigned humility, he was saying that my father was going to die anytime from then. He called him Thomas as he said that, because he identified him in that way as a doctor. Maybe it would have shown me he cared in any way if he had addressed him to my mother as your husband and to me as your father. But I bet he didn't think that meant anything. Thomas he was, just a vegetated man whose body was about to be whisked away to the mortuary as another cold body whose functioning had stopped. I mean, he surely saw that all the time so this was no big deal. I actually took no offence at his demeanor.

I recall as we took turns with my mother sleeping on the floor at Aga Khan, the previous night as I woke up to start my shift, she had asked me:

'In that remote village you people come from, how are we going to live without Daddy?'

My mother has such a strong personality: I have not seen the kind of resilience she has. She doesn't break easily. That night though, I saw how vulnerable she was when she asked me that question. I don't know if she wanted an answer, or if she just wanted to get it out of her chest. In her eyes, I saw for the first time what it meant to hit rock bottom. She was on the cusp of misery. She knew her husband was dying and she was going to have to pick up the pieces and keep moving on. I was there, but I bet she knew this was always going to be her cross to carry. I can imagine what was going through her mind at that moment. I know she felt really alone at that moment and she knew her life ahead was ruined moving forward.

We will survive: I told her that night.

I do not know why I told her that, because I did not believe we would. My father had been everything to my family and even to the extended family and his loss was going to leave the biggest hole in the Were family. I suppose I told my mother that we would survive because seeing her vulnerable made me feel that she was yearning for hope, and I had to give her that by making that a hopeful moment. I did not even believe there was a chance we were going to survive without my father. I could see the harsh pain we were about to experience if that happened, but I knew if my father died then I had to give my mother my shoulder to learn on moving forward. I knew she needed a shoulder if only for that moment and so I handed out my shoulder to her to learn on.

We will survive however hard it will be.

I remembered my dad, the man who had now vegetated in his bed, only a week earlier telling me - 'Death cannot be treated omera. Only diseases are treated.' Looking back, I suppose my father put himself in a space that he expected any eventuality. Sometimes, he would ask some of the people who came to see him:

'What is wrong with death? Is it not part of this life we live?We will all become history at some point'

I remember the day his close friend Mr. Odhiambo visited and he told him:

'You live and die. That's how the world works'

We were going to have to survive whatever the case.

"Omera," I shouted as I tried to pry open his eyes the morning of 22nd March 2017. All through the previous day, his eyes had been wide open but he had no visual response at all. It is like he was not seeing anybody or anything because he made no response even if you waved close to his eyes. Now his pupils were dilated but his eyes were quickly shutting down. He was finding it challenging keeping them open and he was massively drooling I had to wipe the saliva off his lips after every minute. I would try force him with a glass of water and he would make an effort to look at me and fail miserably at it.

Up until this moment, I do not know if, on the last two days, he could see or not, because there was no point he looked me in the eyes or made any response to my attempts to keep him alert. Sometimes I greatly shook him to try and elicit a response from him. Especially when

I greatly shook him, there was no response. He just kept drooling and shutting his eyes in tacit slow motions. I remembered all the times I had used the word cabbage to describe living people in my essays.

On the night of 21st, in a fit of anger, he had called me Richard, his younger brother who had visited him only two days earlier. And I had shaken him and told him 'An Adol, wuodi' (I am Adol, your son} and my mother had quickly admonished me and told me 'you should take any identity that he gives you. He does not know who we are anymore. This is not the moment to be a baby. All you have to do is accept and listen'.

Take whatever name he calls you, because he could want to tell that identity something and you are the one who is around to take that message. Do not contest it. Do not get emotional about it. It turns out he was actually asking his brother to take him to die in his home. Only, he was asking me. He could have asked me to take him home. My mother has seen so many people die she was sort of numb to the process of death. Until then, I had not and it is unfortunate my father was being my first nasty experience with a dying person. And he was looking at me and thinking I was somebody else. He could have asked me to take him home and I would have.

I broke down.

I had been so desperate for him to realize I was calling him Daddy and at least respond in any way: even by shrugging his shoulders. I was so desperate to be my father's son as he died. It's all I wanted at that moment, to be his son. I did not want to be the okil he was calling me or to discuss local politics with him as we often did when we met. I just wanted to be his first born son and for him to know he was leaving behind a capable son. You go through life taking for granted certain momentary pleasures and then when it comes to naught, you do not get that grand pleasure anymore. I just wanted to be a son. In the whole wide world, all I wanted that day was to be his boy.

It is gut-wrenching how your own father can die not knowing who you are. A friend of mine took his mother on a spiritual journey in the last quarter of 2018 because she had developed dementia and could not recognize any of her children and I shuddered to imagine what that did to them. She is still alive at the moment of going to press and I constantly feel the agony of the family. She goes on long trances too just reminiscing because she is constantly hoping one day she will recognize them again and that it is not a train too far gone. I cannot imagine how much it would break me if my mother lived for a protracted period of time without being able to recognize who I was. It would be the typical case of what heartbreak is.

I can remember several instances that I had been proud to be my father's son, but the truth is that they were very fleeting moments: moments that came and went without

me giving them much thought. Even in his modesty, my father got vain at times. Like there was this moment he told me he had written for the Siaya Governor a speech at one of their workshops and he felt so proud of himself he said he should have been the governor then. What was the need of having a Governor who could not come up with a simple speech? I concurred.

I grew up thinking my father was rich because he gave us all the comfort we ever needed growing up. We did not lack anything we asked for and yet he was not rich at all. The man raised us on a salary of less than Kshs 30000 a month and yet we all went to the best of schools and never lacked anything we needed and at no time did he crumble. He survived on loans after loans just so we could have it all. My father was my hero by all standards as I grew up and I was extremely proud of him at all times and I wanted to grow into a proud son and I had wrongly assumed that our destinies were tied together and he would outlive me in any case. I thought I was always going to have time to pay him back for all the struggles.

He is still my hero and I am still proud of him and I know very little ever changes in the grand scheme of things.

At that moment though, I only wanted to hang onto the last moments of being a son, to simply have my father acknowledge me as he floated away. To say this is my son in whom I am well proud. So badly, I wanted to have my father back. Two days after being in hospital I remember a friend had come to visit and asked him if I was his youngest brother and he said "this is my son". I wanted us to stay rooted in that moment forever. I wanted to hear him call me Adol or Ong'er or Omera one last time. I could work with anything. Anything that acknowledged me being a son or someone he was proud of too. It was not coming. It did not come.

That's why on that evening when I realized I had lost my dad to his pain, I left Aga Khan to go for a walk in an attempt to breathe. Kisumu, and I will take the flak for this, is still a very basic metropolis, and there are very few places you can go to draw in air unlike the parks in Nairobi, other than the grimy, crowded and boring Oginga Odinga grounds or one of the restaurants and bars. Or the Imperials and Acacias that tower the city. Kisumu is still the brother that insists on joining the table of men even before coming of age. I decided to just take a walk round the Central Business District instead.

I barely remember how I slipped into Choppies Supermarket and bought myself a bag of Tropical Cheese and Onion crisps: thinking chewing something would help stop the way my heart was really pounding. It did not. I hastily branched into the Oginga Odinga grounds and snaked my way back to Aga Khan thinking I would lose breath before I got there and I would surprise everybody by dying before my father did because I was dramatically shaking at this point. I was in quite a funk

that evening. I was fast losing breath and my body was sort of growing really numb: I was feeling as if my body was collapsing into itself. It was a repulsive feeling that I had never had before and this is also because I had never had breathing problems before too. I was also feeling quite lightheaded and dizzy and I was hallucinating that I was fainting.

I was collapsing, literally and literary.

At Aga Khan, I slipped into the male cloakrooms and locked myself in to cry. During our period at the hospital, those washrooms saw me cry so many times before but that day I recollect how I was crying so loudly I could not stop even after I heard someone getting in who luckily did his business and went away. I was short of wailing. You do not realize what kind of space will be a chamber pot that will be a harbor for you when you hit rock bottom until it is. The thing I learnt with male washrooms in hospital is that they were the only safe spaces for men to let it out in that hospital environment. I remember the first time one of my uncles- Richard- visited and saw his brother in such a vulnerable state he left the ward in a hush for the washrooms: only to come back with his eyes so inflamed I knew he'd gone to cry. I could see it in his puffed eyes.

I was not alone.

I cried so much at Aga Khan in the run up to the passing on of Japuonj I left that place feeling so dry on the day

he actually died. I could not even muster the tears on that day. I really wanted to, because he died holding my hands. When a man dies holding your hands, even if he is not your father, it is enough to make you break down. I even tried to summon tears after my mum leaped onto my chest sobbing.

I didn't.

I simply looked at him and asked him "Japuonj why?".

So what is this all about Jakom?

My mum fell so hard on my chest and began to wail I thought I would follow suit because I had never seen her that vulnerable. I didn't. I couldn't. That previous night, I had decided not to sleep at the hospital. I looked at my father and noticed that the same way he was gasping for breath: that same gasping was happening to me too. I was breathing like the dying man right in front of me. There was so much pain coming from my lungs as they constricted. What was wrong with me? I remember telling my mother I was done sleeping at the hospital and I would be spending that night out of the hospital. I told Daddy a feeble bye and crept out of the room at about 9pm in the night and went to sleep thinking it would be all good and yet still hoping against hope in my tiny corner.

Until my mother woke me up at 5am.

'Get here now. This man may not make it past 8am.

Don't even shower.'

I figured loss was on its way. And I was already being hit by all the three elements of pessimism that I later realized are beautifully discussed by the interesting psychologist Martin Seligman:

"Personalization — the belief that we were at fault (I felt at that moment that I had let my father down in a big way. Had we really tried our best to save him? It was a gush of guilt running down my system. That we had not done enough. That we had not been enough.);

Pervasiveness — the belief that an event will affect all areas of our life (what were we going to do now without a father and a husband to my mum, what was our lives supposed to look like now without a father. Was there life without that man that was now dying and yet he had represented all our lives? How we were going to survive now that we had no father or someone that had dedicated his life to taking care of us);

Permanence — the belief that the aftershocks of the event will last forever because of the permanence of death is actually really unbearable (Did life really matter anymore? What was life really worth anymore? If my dad was dead, what was remaining that meant anything in this world. Who was remaining that would take his part? Nothing was ever going to be the same again, and nothing mattered anymore. I do not think I want to live anymore. I cannot live anymore.)."

It was such a dark abyss moment. The pain hits you immediately. Joan Didion said that grief has no distance. It comes in waves, paroxysms, sudden apprehensions that weaken the knees and blind the eyes and obliterates the dailines of life. It does not wait for you to be ready when it hits. That aptly describes what I was going through at that moment. I was in the shower crying as I felt sorry for myself. I figured if he was dying, then he could as well go ahead with it when I was away.

I sent a text message to one of my closest friends.

> "My father is dying. I don't know what will happen, but I think I will be fine. I hope I will be fine. I will try to be fine. I will be fine."

And then I left the house and went to the hospital to wait for my father to die. He did not die before 8am. He gave us three more hours. And then he called it a life.

And that marked the end of an era and we got sucked into an unending cusp of misery.

My Mothers Grief

I love my mother to a fault. I don't think there is anybody I will ever love more in my life. As my father miserably died at Aga Khan, my mother was awfully helpless: and it was about to get worse because she was in reality about to become a hapless victim of grief. I could see it from very early on when he had just been admitted as an in-patient at the hospital. I could tell she knew this was never going to have a good ending. Looking back, I could also hear it in her voice from the many times she had called previously to tell me he was not in good shape. She knew he was dying and it was only a matter of time before she became a widow and lived the rest of her life all alone, something she clearly had not signed up for when she married Tom. As she sat by his bedside helping him to a serving of an apple or a glass of juice, she unsuccessfully tried to mask her worst fears.

She every so often asked him if he actually wanted to die, and sometimes this happened as I sat right across from them on the other side of the bed. Whenever the doctor came in to his ward cubicle, she would ask me to leave and wait outside until when the doctor was done briefing them. And then she told me zilch when I tried to prod her about the ward round. I always insisted on having the right to know what was going on and she always found a diversion to my obstinacy. I now know she was always trying to protect me, because I was still the little boy she was paying school fees for. This was new to our family.

When my father had started to vegetate after about ten days in hospital, she ordered my younger brother not to come to the hospital anymore. She lied to him that the doctors had said nobody should visit him any longer. She gave no reason for how a son would be denied to see their father in hospital but I bet she expected no challenge from Ian either. When my brother asked me what was going down, I actually told him to get to hospital because the old man was wasting away fast. I told him this was his father, and if he did not come in time, it would be too late much like how our mother had been telling us when we were still in Nairobi. This man is doing quite poorly, I remember repeating to him quite a few times that evening.

With the benefit of hindsight, again, I now know all she was trying to do was protect her last born. I do not know what was really going through her mind in those instances, but I always know she somehow knew he was not going to make it out of that hospital bed. It may have just been a thought she harbored at that point, but she took it very seriously. She occasionally sang to him songs I only hear sang at memorials and yet he was still very much alive, only vegged out. There are long moments she left to go for a walk and I always know she went to cry. I know because I also took those walks and I always understood her. Her husband was in point of fact dying. Once, on those last days, when we stayed back at night to take care of the old man as I have recounted elsewhere in this book, she asked me how we would survive alone back in the remote village that is Masiro incase our father died.

Masiro is in the back of the beyond of Ugenya. It is an extremely remote and primitive village that borders Luo land and the beginning of the Mumias side of Luhya land. It is like an afterthought, because not much happens there. It is a place with little dreams and a population that has made peace with poverty and despondency. It is a community where the only constant is life and things like ambition or growth do not actually bother most of the people. We come from a place that would inspire very little in anybody. It is also where my father came from and beat all odds to become a successful man by any standards. There, he had also built a beautiful house that he had planned to settle in with my mother after retirement and he was actually planning to commit to an early retirement based on a conversation we had previously had.

They had not finished building their house and I think my mother knew that that was seemingly now a long shot by all standards. So I imagine the future my mum pictured at that moment of her in that place all alone and how bleak it must have looked to her. She could not begin to imagine how she was supposed to even make it. We were all already grown up and by any measure we would not be spending more than a few days at the village during holidays. Our lives were always going to move on and we had so many options that she was never going to have. These were facts neatly stacked up against her.

On the flip side of things, retirement was sneaking up on her and so that meant moving back to the village was quite a foreseeable reality that stared her smack in the face. I tend to think when she asked me that question, she dreaded the very idea of what being in that environment portended for her. I think she was looking back at the last 28 years she had spent with my dad under his wings, and she could not fathom going ahead without him. I know it greatly worried her. It significantly worried me too. This was looking like an Armageddon of sorts. The world was clearly conspiring against her.

Later on, most of her fears would become true on the

hostility that she would face in the middle of her grief. Like I told you, I come from a very primitive village and the system being largely patriarchal, I always understood how that was bound to happen and I always knew she was able to take care of herself when it got to that. My mother is no pushover. That she was always going to surmount that spectacle never worried me at all. I say it very lightly but my mother is the personification of resilience.

When the doctor called us on the morning my father was to die and said that his situation was quite grave and not much would be done anymore, my mother showed no particular sentiment. She did not seem to want to clutch at straws. She didn't plead or beg them to take him to the Intensive Care Unit or to try and help him further. In fact, when the issue of being transferred to the ICU came up, it is my mother who said that it was not necessary. She simply told the doctor to 'Let the Lord have his way' and requested that they allow us spend his last moments with him as his family and she went ahead and signed some consent forms as I grumbled next to her: 'You can't be serious'.

But that was not the first moment my mother surrendered on that morning. At about six in the morning, my mother had called my uncle frantically to ask me to go to the hospital because she was particular that my father was not going to make it past eight that morning. She asked me not to shower or even iron my clothes but head to the hospital immediately. Her voice sounded quite worrisome from what I could let my emotions process in that whirlpool of confusion. She was being quite alarmist and I had to do as she had said. I slept a little more though because I had decided that I did not want to be there as he died.

In retrospect, I think she wanted me to be there when he died because she was afraid he would die on her alone.

He did not make it past that day, but he beat the 8am deadline.

He disappointed her on that front.

She was not in the ward cubicle when he died, and I remember her not being amongst the first few to know he had coasted away already. When she came into the cubicle and I shouted to her that he was gone and she saw he was gone the very first thing she did was she went and removed the wedding ring on his finger, clenched back his fingers and then turned away as if to leave. Then she turned right back and fell on my chest and made a really shrill but short wail.

I hugged and embraced her and I felt a really sharp sting hit my stomach.

It must have been a really painful moment for her and she stuck on my chest for a little longer coming to terms with the finality of death: death of the man she had loved till death literally did them part. I cannot imagine what

she felt at that very moment because I cannot describe what I felt at that moment. I could not cry, so I just held her. She had lost a lifelong companion, I had only lost my father and so my grief was still so many lower levels than hers. I do not say grief can be quantified or in any way compared, but I know what hit my mother on that day was indescribable. I do not discount any sort of grief but I know that day broke my mothers' heart more than it did mine. On top of my grief, I was devastated on her behalf.

He was actually gone now.

It was no longer just a premonition she had.

At that moment, I saw my mother extremely helpless and vulnerable just as I had seen my father a few days earlier at the facility. Five days earlier, at about 5:30pm, my father will be asked to go in for his Computerized Tomography (CT) Scan. He will be asked by the nurse if he needs a wheelchair to help him down the ramp and he will say he is fine. Classic Omondi Were. So I will take him down to the lab and after the scan he will ask me to escort him outside the wards to see the sky. We will make some small banter at the bench outside Aga Khan Hospital Kisumu and after twenty minutes head back to the ward. About midway up the ramp, he will tell me he is exhausted and he has lost breath. He will ask me to help him get to his ward room up the stairs so he could rest. That is the first time in my life I would see my father extremely helpless and vulnerable that he would ask me to do something for him. So we will hold shoulders and I will slowly walk him up the ramp. What he will not know is that that would be the last day he will see the sky, for he will begin to die the very next day.

On that tragic morning though, my mothers' vulnerability lasted for very few minutes because soon enough she dried her tears and began being the leader of the tribe that she always had been. She began organizing how the body would be taken to the morgue and what the costs would amount to: she began consulting on the days that were viable for a burial; she began organizing how we would get home that afternoon and what we would eat for supper: she was all over the phone informing her friends and those of my dad that he was already gone. Like me, she would begin the process of transferring the grief to everybody else other than herself. It was the easiest way to deal with it at that time because the opposite would be to break down in front of everybody that was looking at her for directions. Yes, we were all looking at her for directions.

My entire life, my mother has always been the strongest woman in the room: the one people fell back to at such moments, and it was chilling to see how at her moment of extreme grief and pain, she still made herself the one people fell back to. She was still that woman. The one people looked at for all manner of directions. In my head, I knew she was still at the denial face of her grief, but

later I realized she was just being the strongest woman in the room because the truth is nobody would have taken up the task had it not been for her. She could not afford to break down at that moment despite the fact that she had all the rights to.

I remember the very next day when we had to go back to the hospital to sort the expenses and she had insisted on going alone and her best friend had insisted that I had to escort her and she flat out refused. "This is the Omondi Were you have with you now. Don't assume you are alone" she told her but she would hear none of it. In the end, I had to go. This is a scene that repeated itself so many times within the first two years that he was gone: so many instances my mother needed my help without actually being comfortable asking for it and I had to always see those moments myself and step up. I understood her though, because she wanted Omondi Were and I was no Japuonj myself. I was her son, and therefore I was always going to remain a little boy in her face.

My mother is grit-personified. Within the next two weeks that preceded the burial, she was constantly on the move trying to organize all she could. At no point did I see her take a step back to grieve and to just have her own time. She never locked herself in a room for any long hours to just let out. Granted, like in the Luo culture, she would wake up at the crack of dawn with other mourners to mourn the departed and they would use that moment to cry and ask questions. I always did too and took a specific corner and really cried and let out the anger and bitterness that I harbored in my chest. I hated God on those days. But that was it because when day dawned it was back to organizing and scheduling and everything else but grief.

At the first hint of daylight, Auma Keya was always on her feet organizing this and planning that. Any spectator would never have known she was the one who was widowed. She never sat anywhere in a black dress welcoming visitors and in constant tears. Visitors found her in her state of activity, constantly in the kitchen and monitoring all the other plans and sometimes even out of home to partake in humdrum tasks such as buying fish in Busia. In any case, even on the burial day, my mother had to be hounded out of home by force and asked to sit down and mourn. One of her best friends literally had to sit next to her to ensure she was in a state of inactivity.

My father had been the quintessential leader of the tribe himself. He was a man of the people and he had impacted on so many lives. People actually really loved Japuonj. It is something I knew but I never really understood the impact of until I saw hundreds upon hundreds of people on his burial day. So many people still walk up to me on this day and say I was at your dads funeral and we even said hi to one another and I can't remember at all. That was a surreal rally. He was a man and a half indeed.

My mother had therefore been determined to bury her friend well and to give him a really befitting send off. She was thus clear on very many things from the word go.

The very first time we sat down as a family to plan for the burial, we were toying around with numbers and we settled on a lean figure of 1000 people and tried to have a budget around that figure. In the final calculations, the budget was coming to around a million shillings and there was a sigh across the room because, like I told you before, I come from Masiro Konya Village. There was thus consensus that even if the entire family contributed down to a penny, we were still in no position to raise even half that amount and my mother had already even sunk into a deeper fleapit of debts and was flat-out hard up. If anything, my parents had been very broke at the time of my fathers' death. We were in great trouble yet one way or another; we bore the responsibility of having to give Daddy a befitting sendoff, befitting the hero he had been. We all didn't know how that was going to happen at that time, but it was sure going to happen. It had to happen.

Later that day, I saw fear in my mother's eyes as she asked me where that kind of money would come from, where we were going to get money to bury Omosh. I encouraged her that something was going to come through. I remember telling her that Daddy had friends all over the place and they were sure going to come through. She just sighed, with great frustration. There

was a fundraiser planned for that coming weekend, I reminded her but she was still quite blue. I could see this matter really worried her. This matter actually worried me more because I knew my father would have done everything possible and moved mountains if it was somebody else who was dead.

Mungu naye ni nani, just a week after that conversation and as I had predicted, a gathering of a few of my fathers' tribe would raise that money and change. Secondary school Principals from different walks of life had been there. His friends from everywhere were there. His family was there. It was so effortless that there was never a rally or some form of coercion to raise that money. In two hours, they had raised more than a million shillings. I knew that day that my father was a man of his own kind. I also knew that I wanted to be the kind of man my dad had been. Or even just half the man. I hope that is a dream I get to achieve, and that I get to be a better version of my father, the version he was becoming before death robbed him from this world. But I know that is a task too tall and I would be proud if as I mention up here, I am merely half the man my old man was. That man had great panache. Tom was impressive!

Death of a close person is an extremely traumatizing affair and it can be even more excruciating if you have to go through the motions of it alone. I am quite grateful for the fact that my mother had a really supportive cast around her. One of her friends was always by her side at any given time before the burial. If it was not Madam Vicky, it was Madam Pamela Nandi or Mrs. Amili or somebody else. She was in no shortage of a shoulder to lean on. There was always a tribe around her and I know she received a lot of love from those people. I know they shielded her from constantly breaking down during that period. Nonetheless, the truth though is that grief is an extremely personal affair because two days after the burial, she remained back alone with her unopened box of grief.

Two weeks after burying our father, we would sit in the living room with my mother to go through some of his documents. His pay slips indicated that he had taken a 2 million loan from the Kenya Commercial Bank the previous year and the arrears were astounding. We both sunk into a hole. What would happen now? She asked me. I told her banks are business and loan facilities must always be repaid so they may seek to take the land or the car or anything available to service what was remaining of the loan and it almost killed her.

It was surprising to me that even as a teacher, my mother has actually never taken a bank loan before and she therefore did not know how they even worked. I was a student so I merely made an assumption from the little I had gleaned from my banking law classes that banks don't renege on their debts owing. She then asked me to call the bank immediately and find out. You can imagine our sigh of relief when we learnt that bank loans based on pay slips as securities are insured and so insurance would pay for them and all we had to do was report to the bank. I saw her cry on that day despite that relief. That would have been a thunderbolt. We did not know if more surprises were on the way.

One week after my father had been buried, my mother called us into the kitchen for a talk. She offered to share with us some of the money she had received during the burial: cash which we gladly accepted considering our financial positions at that time was quite bad. It had been a messy two weeks since my father had died. We all felt that was a really considerate thing for her to do at that time. Ian and I also used this opportunity to ask for a few more things. Ian had just gotten a job as a journalist and therefore made a plea for his laptop and phone and I asked for his other phone and Ipad. We had primarily asked for these gadgets because my mother was a self-declared technophile and we knew she definitely had no use for this electronics.

We were wrong, because she went on a long rant immediately we made the ask. Our father had not even been on the soil for one week and we were already in a rush to share his things. We did not look like people who were grieving but opportunists. Did we even care that we had lost him or we looked at this as a moment to gain? Did we want her to also die? My mother can be a tad dramatic when she needs to be. We had failed to read the signs. I remember getting very cross with her

at that moment without even stopping to understand where she was coming from. I took offence because I had lost my brightest star at that moment and she was making it look like she was the only one who had lost a loved one and was in the pits. I had failed to read what was happening.

She was saying you cannot begin to erase my memories of him at this moment!

I only came to understand her position at that time when a year down the road she had not given out even a sock from his closet apart from those I had stolen. I think she was clutching at the very memory of him using everything of his he left behind. I think his clothes and books and gadgets were the very few things she felt would keep him still present. We looked at the laptop as if it was a perishable product and yet my mum looked at it as if it was an embodiment of his presence in the room. We looked at those gadgets like they were just simply electronic gadgets: she saw him in them. Even at the time of going to press with this, over three years later, his closet stands tall. I remember the last time I asked for some pair of shoes and she told me they were his best. It took me such a long time to gasp the very fact that his belongings signified his metaphysical presence and disposing them would be akin to erasing his very existence.

The other time I saw my mother seriously go off tangent

was when Ian came home with his friends who had not been able to attend the burial. Like ideal millennials, they were not coming home for a mourning session: they coming to celebrate the life of the old man. While at it, they were also using this opportunity to tour Nyanza as most of them had not been on that side of the country. I totally understood them. My mother had on the flip side however expected a convoy coming to simply mourn Japuonj and was greatly disappointed in the amount of fun the gentlemen seemed to be having in this trip. For starters, they got home at 10pm on the first day which had been extremely wrong by any standards, give it to her. The next day, they would eat at home and then leave for a tour and pass by the bar to take one for the road. Later in the night, they gathered in the tent and began telling endless stories and when after midnight they had not gone to sleep, my mother called Ian and flew off the handle. They left before the sun was out.

In her burial speech, my mother recounted how my father had seduced her for two years because she always took a long time to make a decision. I fully agreed with her on the aspect of decision making. She has this uncanny habit of taking ages to make a simple decision on literally even otherwise ordinary issues. In contrast, my father made his decisions on his feet. He had quite the spring on his walk, that man. My mother, on the other end, has a difficult time deciding on even the most basic of issues like changing the furniture material or

what color of paint to use. We have sort of gotten used to it by now.

One thing however my mother did not falter to make an immediate decision on was the fact that we would have an in memoriam in a year. In the Luo tradition however there was the pending memorial of my grandfather which had to be done before that of my father could materialize. She was always particular that Japuonj would have wanted his sao done immediately. She would therefore persuade the family to organize the memorial of Mzee early on and on 27th January 2018 we all gathered back at Masiro and had the memorial of Mzee Michael Were Atogo. It was a somber moment reliving the life of Mzee and this thereafter paved the way for Japuonjs' memorial.

On the 23rd of March that year, it would be exactly one year after the passing on of my dad at Ward 1 Bed 10 of the Agha Khan Hospital. It would be an extremely long year but we had all made it, with our grief and broken parts notwithstanding. I remember earlier on seeing the toll grief had taken on the physical appearance of my mother and shuddering if she would make it. Before that day, she would ask me to take an advert at the Daily Nation and pen an anniversary message and a Thank You note.

IN LOVING MEMORY/ FIRST ANNIVERSARY.
THOMAS OMONDI WERE
18TH AUGUST 1963 – 23RD MARCH 2017

Dear Daddy,

Today marks a year since the curtain fell on your act.
Though you are forever gone, our loving memory of you
cannot fade away. You remain as a deeply engraved part
of our hearts and we still highly cherish your strength,
vision and generosity.

We thank God for the impactful moment we had you
in our lives, and for giving us the grace and strength to
endure the emptiness of losing you in our lives. Because
we shared in your moment, our lives will be fuller and our
love deeper.

You are dearly missed by your entire family and friends
and especially by your loving wife, Joan: your children
Ian, Sharon, Emily, Effie, Evans and Austine.

Your absence is a silent grief: your life a beautiful
memory.

The Omondi Were Family would like to extend its sincere
gratitude to those who have offered their generous
support to us from then until now.

Be Blessed.

"I am the resurrection and the life, he who believes in me will live, even though he dies" John 11:25.'

On that day, we would all gather at St Joseph's Catholic Church Ugunja for a morning mass where my mother would donate a pew to the church in his memory. Later in the afternoon we would go to Masiro and pray on his grave and just spend the afternoon together with him as his nuclear family. That day was filled with so much love even amongst ourselves I remember thinking later in the evening that we would make it out of the darkness. My mother would however insist on staying back in the evening as we went back to our residence in Ugunja. I think about that day a lot because I know it was one of the days in a really long time when I was actually happy and surrounded by people I greatly loved.

That same year, we would organize his memorial on the 18th of August 2018. It would have been his 54th birthday on that day. My mother had chosen that date specifically because it had coincided with his birth date. She had never consulted anybody on that date and actually only reminded us it was his birthday during the memorial celebrations. For one more time that year therefore, we would gather at the Omondi Were boma to break bread and remember the life of a man who had lived such an illustrious but short life. It was a really beautiful ceremony and it was heartwarming how yet one more time the entirety of the tribe Japuonj had gathered around him came to celebrate him. I keep saying he was

a really striking man because we received so much love when he passed on and long after he had been buried. I do not believe it would have been the same if he wasn't.

My mother has gone through great motions of grief. I took a time off when my father died to spend some time with her despite her protestations. For around two mouths, I followed her around and helped her do a few things. She was always feigning strength but I always saw right through her whenever she needed help. Once she went back to work, I took my next bus to Nairobi too hoping that she was going to be fine. For a while, we never spoke I assume because we were actually trying to be busy to avoid the grief. Whenever we spoke, I could always hear the strain in her voice. The truth however is there was almost always nothing I would do and she always dealt with her own issues. Today, I am awed at how she surmounted that difficult moment if she has surmounted it that is. I am aware of the fact that even if she hasn't as I sometimes see, there is only so much I can help with considering my mother's poor attitude to asking for help too. I however do not doubt that she will pull through.

For years now after the passing on of my father, the gap has been very minimal. My mother has always come through. We have not lacked because he is not there and bills have not gone unpaid or school fees not completed in time. In her own way, she struggles to ensure the loss of my father has not meant there was any sort of end in

our lives as we have always known it. Like most of our old school African mothers, she is not the most outward loving of people but I constantly see how she shows me and my siblings time and again the love and that she is a breastplate we can always rely on. Like with my father, I go through life knowing I have my mother as my new last line of defence. I hope we someday get to pay her back for the years she has sacrificed her happiness and joy for us: for all the times she has not been able to live her own life and make her own choices. In his absence, I want her to know I intend to forever take care of her.

In my father's death, I want to remain my mother's son.

In The Eye of the Storm

Grief is certainly more like a country too; everybody seems to have a different experience of it when it comes full circle. I saw my mother put on a brave face during the first few months of grieving and sometimes thought she had managed to move on quite speedily. At the same time, I could see how her weight was shuttling towards zero for someone who was already so skinny in her stature. I could also see how withdrawn my brother had become even as he tried to get back to living his normal life as he had just landed a new job at Royal Media Services. My sister Effie did not speak for shit: you just saw her moving around the house doing whatever it is she was on and flipping all sorts of Nigerian movie channels on the TV. My eldest sister Emily had pulled a disappearing act presumably to handle her grief in her own way.

As I sat to write this, around two years four months after my father had long gone to rest, I remember asking myself if there were things between my father and myself that had gone unsaid or undone. I wondered if in the eye of the storm I had actually had the right conversations with him. I had always assumed I would have the rest of time to converse with my father and especially because our relationship was slowly beginning to grow into the atypical father-son relationship I never imagined it would blossom into. We were becoming buddies. I was beginning to fully identify with him as my true guide and I knew I owed him a lot for the man I was becoming. It is no wonder therefore I was asking myself if there were things that had gone unraveled in our relationship that in any case was just ideally taking off.

Right off the bat, I realized that I had failed myself during the pendency of our hospital stay by never engaging my father deeply on how he felt about how his life had turned out. I can say it is because I never imagined for one that he was dying at that moment but that as an excuse would still fall flat on its face. We both had the time to talk about a few things and we could have talked about stuff as deep as I would have gone: he was always in a talking mood on some days when he felt a little better. Looking back, it was probably the only opportunity in our whole lives that I was presented with to have such a conversation with him, and this had nothing to do with whether he was going to die or recover. This was a moment I would have gotten to know my father and I did not. The failure to do so therefore has to follow me as my uncharted trauma.

I remember failing to ask him the one question that I know for a fact could have given me some sort of closure once he passed on. I say this without necessarily believing that closure is an antidote to grief, but I think closure pacifies the stinging process of grief. When in a state of grief, you need something that can help quell the anger. You need to move on with life without holding onto the moments of extreme pain and anger that life conspired to thrust your way at some point. In the end, don't we all seek some form of closure when trauma hits us? An end we can hold onto. A point of memory that we can keep latching on to give us hope as we attempt to continue going through the journey of life. Don't we all hope for such ends?

On the 18th of March, when Dr. Okell had suggested we have him temporarily discharged from the hospital due to the piling hospital bill and wait for the biopsy results at home because they were going to take a week as the samples had to be sent to Nairobi for the pathology, he probably knew that my dad was not going to make it past that week. He knew there was nothing else he was going to be able to do. My father was eerily quite easy about it; he actually asked us to go home and come back when the biopsy results were out. He was of the view that we would be wasting hospital bills without any treatment

regimen going on. Take me home, he snapped.

I took great umbrage and told him we were going nowhere in his sorry state.

"In the state you are in, we can't leave the hospital. Home will not do any good to you. If you are to recover, this is where you recover."

"Are you a doctor? If a doctor has said I can go home, who are you? Take me home Omera."

"I am the one with you here and you can't even go to the toilet alone now you want to go home to do what exactly?"

"If I am to die my friend, I will do so even if you take me to England."

"So, do you want to die then?"

"It is people who die. If I die I die. In any case, if I were to die today, what don't you people have? What have I not done for you? What do you want me to point to you where it is? Have I not been a good father to you guys? Is there anything you would have wanted from me that I did not provide to you people?"

On that day, my father broke my heart. He seemed to be surrendering yet the battle was just beginning. He seemed worn out enough that he was contemplating death and he saw absolutely no issue with it. I remember that day almost every day of my life and my heart still sinks because maybe that could be the day my father actually did begin to die. Maybe that is the day he actually died.

{"Let's talk about you for a second now that you do not fear death. If you were to die today, would you be satisfied and fulfilled with the life you have lived? Are you happy with how your life panned out?"}

They say hindsight is 20/20 and it for sure hits home because I didn't ask him that last question when he asked about what we would lack even if he died. If I remember well I know I really wanted to have that conversation with him. I almost did. But I didn't. I felt it would have been greatly inconsiderate and insensitive of me so I backed down and took a walk. I acquiesced because -in his death bed- that is not a question I felt a son should ask a father who sacrificed almost everything for them. I felt that was quite a cruel question. Maybe I also did not ask him because I would not have wanted to hear the spot on answer to that question. What would I have done if he had been unfulfilled and dissatisfied? I cannot claim to have an idea what the true answer to that question was, but I am not sure the answer would have been a rosy one either. I am not sure that the answer was one I could have dealt with had he blurted it out.

It haunts me however that I failed to ask Japuonj the

one question that perchance would have given me a semblance of peace after his death. I struggled so much with that question long after his death. I considered it as probably the most existential question of his life. I kept asking myself if there were any clues that would show me that my father had been a fulfilled and happy man as at the time he was dying. I kept rummaging through some of my memories of him to assure myself he had lived a worthy life. Most of my mind at that moment was full of the mundane memories we shared, especially during the school holidays and festivities. I was keen on finding anything to clutch on as his joie de vivre moments. That proved such a futile exercise.

My truth is that I don't think he felt fulfilled or even remotely happy on that death bed.

I will most likely keep on living assuming he didn't die a happy man.

Weeks and months later as I discovered snippets of things about him, I realized my father may have died the most unfulfilled man in the world. It was all I could see whenever I turned my head to look into his life and his correspondences and his documents. There were lots of times he had been struggling with one thing or the other. Some of the things I bumped on by chance constantly showed me that there was more to Japuonj than we had lived through. Maybe it was because I was searching for the very aspects that showed disillusion instead of the positive aspects or memories of him that were way many and in the open. I also think it is a very difficult thing to quantify happiness while sadness lays itself out. I for instance took it with great blues the fact that in close to ten years he was living and servicing one loan facility or the other. In some of those years, they were several facilities from various institutions that showed he was always on a financial limb.

But I will never know unless I had asked him that question that easy Saturday morning of March 2017. I have to live my life knowing I will never get to know the answer to that question. I have to live my life believing he was at least content. I know for sure that my father did not live his life as a grumpy or disenchanted man. He showed up when he needed to and at no point did he fail to fulfill his duty. My mind keeps shifting to that scene in Fences acted out by Denzel Washington when he is telling his son that as a father he does everything to him because he owes him and not because of love or any other consideration. My father fulfilled every single duty he could possibly have owed his family. I wonder of that at least gave him some joy in his heart.

On the flip side, I do not know if my father felt we appreciated him enough at the time of his demise. I know I always told him every single Father's Day that I would never have wished for a better dad and I loved him so much but that was just it. I never in one instance bought him even a shirt to say thank you and I know for a fact neither did any of my siblings. As for my mother, they had their deal when they got married and so that was their business. The truth though is my father dedicated everything he could possibly have to us but we never got the opportunity to pay back. I remember telling myself that I wanted to buy my father a collection of the most expensive Whiskeys during his retirement as he lounged in his boma. I also promised myself to buy him a better car once I had fulfilled the promise to buy my mother one (of which I am four years late now). There were a couple of things I intended to do, but nothing I was doing at the time, not even an ink pen to sign his school checks with. I knew he was going to live forever. This too shall be my trauma to deal with.

The essence of this chapter is not in any case to propound any unfortunate grand notion that my father was an unhappy man by any standards as he lived. My father lived his life like a candle in the wind and I know like with any human being there were highs and lows with his lowest being the death of his father and his highest being when I was born (mic drop). I just think he was not ready to die when it happened because he still had a whole life ahead of him. I know for a fact because there are certain things we discussed endlessly in the years before death struck and even while in hospital. He wanted to immediately retire from teaching to start his own businesses and to begin living his life for himself. He had asked me to register a few businesses for him. I think he also wanted to begin having his me time after over thirty years of being an unappreciated civil servant in Kenya: quite the thankless job it seemed.

What he didn't know was that that was never going to happen.

In The Fog of Grief

In the weeks after my father passed on I read, unendingly, on grief. I had decided from very early on after the demise that I would try handling my grief very academically. I gobbled readings on what it meant to grieve, and how the grieving process allowed someone to transition and let go eventually as the society oft-required. You were not supposed to grieve forever, I had been told.

My friend Dickens sent me a text just two months after my father had died and told me that I was grieving for an unnecessarily long period of time. He advised me to let go and move on with my life because what had happened had happened and I was unable to do anything about it. He warned me that being pointlessly beholden to memories of the past was me holding my life back and it was not going to benefit me in any way. He offered all this advice because I had posted a picture of my father on my Instagram account two months after he had passed on. Life has to move on, he countered.

I turned to books, the one thing I knew I could turn to with searing commitment. Grief is not something people share, I already knew, but I wanted to find out how other people had dealt with their grief and how they had managed to move past it and the pointers they were giving out in their books and articles. I wanted to learn from those who had been stuck in a rut before, and still found their way out. Grief is a walk you are obligated to make alone, but even such walks need a thread to hang onto. I wanted to find out how one got back on top of water. Like with this book, I merely wanted to see how people got back to their true selves after loss. At the time, I had assumed those books provided a formula on dealing with grief and were unlike this book that merely shares my experiences staring at an abyss. At that time, I thought it was a necessary forage and I knew it was going to pay off and I would come up from those books and have a roadmap as to how I was going to mourn my dad and for exactly how long.

I re-read Carla Malden's In Memoriam 'After Image' immediately my pops passed on. I had read it just one year earlier. It is a harrowing yet striking narration on believing in love even in the midst of grief. It is a gripping book on the nexus between grief and love. Carla writes on how the one man she had grown to really love would go on to fight colon cancer unsuccessfully: a pain-ridden eleven months those would be to herself and her family. She writes so beautifully about death as an awakening on how much more love she would never be able to expend again, ever. She writes quite elegantly about loving her husband to the very last minute he lost his breath, and then loving him even more posthumously. On the day my father passed on, I made a mental note that I was going to read Malden again.

The first time I had read the book I had been a third year student at the University. I remember being so consumed with anger at why such a young person had to face such a cruel and excruciating death, and at how despite being overly sad about losing her flame, Malden had been able to really write a book on grief like it was a book on love. In point of fact, it was a book on love. Initially, I had read the book like I had read a Game of Thrones paperback and it was George R.R Martin killing off one of my favorite characters. The thing is that I had read the book like I was reading fiction and such a topic was a distant experience: at this time tragedy had not struck me yet. I had picked the book from the streets for a paltry one hundred shillings because I had loved the prologue and I thought I needed to read the story.

Carla Malden writes so blindingly on her journey losing a soul mate in the most painful of deaths. It's the first book in a long time I closed myself in my room and clenched my fists and cried. This was because I was now reading it for the second time and my father had died and I had turned into Carla Malden and there were even more sweeping emotions engulfing me at that time as I flipped the pages. It is me people now looked at with sympathy. There are things that happen to other people and you feel extremely sorry for them and pat them on the back with sorrow and tell them it shall be fine, and then those very things happen to you and people are feeling extremely sorry for you and patting you on the back with sorrow and telling you it will be fine. At that moment, because you know it shall not be fine, it brings you down to the edge of a precipice.

Stoically, Malden quips:

> "Like love, grief is simple. It is all consuming and uncomplicated".

It is just grief. There is not a single day that I have not remembered my father in one way or another. The truth is, after three years now, not all the days I have been miserable about it. Some days therefore his memory brings distant joy for the kind of life he lived. Some days it is all gloom and doom but it is those days that are in the minority as my life takes the forward march. Grief really is uncomplicated because all it demands is your attention and presence. And then you have to deal with what it puts in front of you. There will be good days and there will be bad days and you have to take a day as it comes. You have to put one foot forward at a time.

After Image is a book I would recommend to anyone who wishes to learn how to live with immense pain and grief that comes as a consequence of losing a very close person by learning that grief is really just love you have to harbor. It's the one book that taught me you can lose someone, without really losing them. They would still be there. After Image is also a book I would recommend to anyone who wants to learn how to write creative non-fiction because Carla Malden weaves her narrations like the expert writer she is. I used it a lot as an after image while I was writing this book and trying to have it laid out.

Years later, when asked about it by a journalist named Trish Crawford why she wrote the book, she calmly said:

> "It's a book about running out of luck. I realize I'm very
> lucky, I have an extraordinary family, spectacular daughter,
> amazing friends and just enough strength, that I didn't
> know I had, to build a life that is productive and filling. I'm
> enjoying new work. I've reclaimed some joy for myself.
> I'm proud of that. I travel, volunteer teaching creative
> writing at a rehab facility. At first I was doing busy work
> but now I'm doing things because they are fulfilling. I am
> not a seeker. I know what's important to me and I know it
> is my relationships."

I remember wondering if my father passing on had been merely us running out of luck too.

Next, I latched on to read Paul Kalanithi's 'When Breath

Becomes Air'. I had seen several recommendations about this book and had also read a Kalanithi article on the Stanford website way before the publishing of the book was even mooted. One of my Facebook friends, Velmah Lumadi, had offered to buy me the book for my 25th birthday and it happened to be a month after my father had passed on. In his death bed, Paul interrogates what life means, and if life really matters in the end if death always wins. While down with a terminal cancer, Paul attempts to find what makes a life worth it in the end. It is a tormenting yet very introspective book on life and death and what there is in between. When I was done, I realized it was never a book about death as much as it was about life. It is a book about gasping for air while immersed in water. Kalanithi observes that 'the fact of death is so unsettling. Yet there is no other way to live'. He goes on a wide foray as to how to find meaning in a life that is meant to end in the end, and sometimes so grotesquely. The book is also an intellectual sojourn on what value literature and science has pondered over life and death. It is a deep book that delves into very complex academic contemplation on time, life and death.

On time, Paul quips that:

> "Time for me is double-edged: Every day brings me further from the low of my last cancer relapse, but every day also brings me closer to the next cancer recurrence — and eventually, death. Perhaps later than I think, but certainly sooner than I desire. There are, I imagine, two

responses to that realization. The most obvious might be an impulse to frantic activity: to "live life to its fullest," to travel, to dine, to achieve a host of neglected ambitions. Part of the cruelty of cancer, though, is not only that it limits your time, it also limits your energy, vastly reducing the amount you can squeeze into a day. It is a tired hare who now races. But even if I had the energy, I prefer a more tortoise like approach. I plod, I ponder, some days I simply persist.

Everyone succumbs to finitude. I suspect I am not the only one who reaches this pluperfect state. Most ambitions are either achieved or abandoned; either way, they belong to the past. The future, instead of the ladder toward the goals of life, flattens out into a perpetual present. Money, status, all the vanities the preacher of Ecclesiastes described, holds so little interest: a chasing after wind, indeed."

When Breath Becomes Air is a haunting yet urgent book in the understanding of the metaphysics of life and death, because it taught me so much about mortality than I would have actually examined myself. I quite enjoyed reading it because I actually read it twice in a span of two weeks, doing nothing else in that period. His wife Lucy writes a beautiful epilogue on the man she knew and narrates how "he confronted death, examined it, wrestled with it and finally accepted it." She goes on to say her lesson from the grief was that our role as human beings is not to fight with fate, but to live through it and to help others do the same. It's about life and death for all of us: a very linear journey. It's about love and loss. But in the end, it's about what mattered to us in the period we had life. What did all the living count for? What did all the living my father did count for? What does all my living count for?

In the twenty two months that he battled Cancer they would decide to have a baby, aptly named Cady, whom Paul would write an immensely lingering tribute to in his book that I feel obligated to share with my reader here.

> "When you come to one of the many moments in life when you must give an account of yourself, provide a ledger of what you have been, and done, and meant to the world, do not, I pray, discount that you filled a dying man's days with a sated joy, a joy unknown to me in all my prior years, a joy that does not hunger for more and more, but rests, satisfied. In this time, right now, that is an enormous thing."

In months that followed, I also paid attention to Sheryl Sandberg, the Facebook poster girl for grief, as she taught others about resilience and overcoming grief. In a cruel twist of fate, Sheryl would lose her husband Dave Goldberg to an accidental blunt force trauma while on holiday to celebrate a friend's birthday in Mexico. She was sleeping as he was exercising at the gym. They were having the perfect life, both Silicon Valley high flyers, when calamity reared its head on them. Some things happen at moments that cannot even be described as the worst. Dave Goldberg faced quite the unexpected end to his life that day in that gym when he collapsed. And behind, he left a broken woman.

Sheryl Sandbergs' post on Facebook at the end of her mourning period remains a great note of reflection to anybody looking at building resilience and bouncing back from anguish. I have debated with myself while writing this on whether to share the story, what parts to share and I sort of know I could not do the cuts and still do it justice. I share long bits of her piece here because I read it so many times after my father died and it lifted my spirits every time I read it, teaching me that grief was not supposed to enervate: and that was one of the reasons I decided to write this book. Sandberg wrote an immortal Facebook post. If you actually can, go read the post on her account this very moment. It is a read I turn to quite regularly to remind myself that grief is not supposed to enervate.

(Sheryl Sandberg Facebook Post on 3rd June 2015)

"
...

I think when tragedy occurs, it presents a choice. You can give in to the void, the emptiness that fills your heart, your lungs, constricts your ability to think or even breathe. Or you can try to find meaning. These past thirty days, I have spent many of my moments lost in that void. And I know that many future moments will be consumed by the vast emptiness as well.

But when I can, I want to choose life and meaning.

...

I have learned that I never really knew what to say to others in need. I think I got this all wrong before; I tried to assure people that it would be okay, thinking that hope was the most comforting thing I could offer. A friend of mine with late-stage cancer told me that the worst thing people could say to him was "It is going to be okay." That voice in his head would scream, How do you know it is going to be okay? Do you not understand that I might die? I learned this past month what he was trying to teach me. Real empathy is sometimes not insisting that it will be okay but acknowledging that it is not. When people say to me, "You and your children will find happiness again," my heart tells me, Yes, I believe that, but I know I will never feel pure joy again. Those who have said, "You will find a new normal, but it will never be as good" comfort me more because they know and speak the truth. Even a simple "How are you?"—almost always asked with the best of intentions—is better replaced with "How are you today?" When I am asked "How are you?" I stop myself from shouting, my husband died a month ago, how do you think I am? When I hear "How are you today?" I realize the person knows that the best I can do right now is to get through each day.

I have learned some practical stuff that matters. Although we now know that Dave died immediately, I didn't know that in the ambulance. The trip to the hospital was unbearably slow. I still hate every car that did not move to the side, every person who cared more about arriving at their destination a few minutes earlier than making room for us to pass. I have noticed this while driving in many countries and cities. Let's all move out of the way. Someone's parent or partner or child might depend on it.

I have learned how ephemeral everything can feel—and maybe everything is. That whatever rug you are standing on can be pulled right out from under you with absolutely no warning. In the last thirty days, I have heard from too many women who lost a spouse and then had multiple rugs pulled out from under them. Some lack support networks and struggle alone as they face emotional distress and financial insecurity. It seems so wrong to me that we abandon these women and their families when they are in greatest need.

I have learned to ask for help—and I have learned how much help I need. Until now, I have been the older sister, the COO, the doer and the planner. I did not plan this, and when it happened, I was not capable of doing much of anything. Those closest to me took over. They planned. They arranged. They told me where to sit and reminded me to eat. They are still doing so much to support me and my children.

I have learned that resilience can be learned. Adam M. Grant taught me that three things are critical to resilience and that I can work on all three. Personalization— realizing it is not my fault. He told me to ban the word "sorry." To tell myself over and over, this is not my fault. Permanence—remembering that I won't feel like this forever. This will get better. Pervasiveness—this does not have to affect every area of my life; the ability to compartmentalize is healthy.

…

I have learned gratitude. Real gratitude for the things I took for granted before—like life. As heartbroken as I am, I look at my children each day and rejoice that they are alive. I appreciate every smile, every hug. I no longer take each day for granted. When a friend told me that he hates birthdays and so he was not celebrating his, I looked at him and said through tears, "Celebrate your birthday, goddammit. You are lucky to have each one." My next birthday will be depressing as hell, but I am determined to celebrate it in my heart more than I have ever celebrated a birthday before.

I am truly grateful to the many who have offered their sympathy. A colleague told me that his wife, whom I have never met, decided to show her support by going back to school to get her degree—something she had been putting off for years. Yes! When the circumstances allow, I believe as much as ever in leaning in. And so many men—

from those I know well to those I will likely never know—
are honoring Dave's life by spending more time with their
families.

I can't even express the gratitude I feel to my family and
friends who have done so much and reassured me that
they will continue to be there. In the brutal moments
when I am overtaken by the void, when the months
and years stretch out in front of me endless and empty,
only their faces pull me out of the isolation and fear. My
appreciation for them knows no bounds.

I was talking to one of these friends about a father-child
activity that Dave is not here to do. We came up with a
plan to fill in for Dave. I cried to him, "But I want Dave.
I want option A." He put his arm around me and said,
"Option A is not available. So let's just kick the shit out of
option B."

Dave, to honor your memory and raise your children as
they deserve to be raised, I promise to do all I can to kick
the shit out of option B. And even though sheloshim has
ended, I still mourn for option A. I will always mourn for
option A. As Bono sang, "There is no end to grief . . . and
there is no end to love." I love you, Dave."

One month after my fathers' death, another gracious
friend from Facebook would send me Sheryl's second
book 'Option B: Facing Adversity, Building Resilience and
Finding Joy' where Sheryl teaches on the lessons on

resilience that her husband's death taught her and what she has learnt about finding joy even in moments of great difficulty. The book is co-written with Adam Grant, a top rated psychologist and Professor at Wharton. It's a critical guide for one to reclaim their lives after momentous loss. Option B is a book packed with great narration and storytelling and which goes on to describe Sandberg's journey through the fog of sadness and anger to her choice to find happiness again. It is a book about learning how to pick up from the ground up once more.

It is a beautifully written study of resilience and how we build it, as well as what it is like to have that resilience tested. It combines research, anecdotes, stories and practical advice to help its readers build strength in surmounting everyday challenges. Despite the paralyzing moments that grief presents in our lives, Sandberg gives you an assurance that you can actually grow from it. "Tragedy breaks down your door and takes you prisoner. To escape takes effort and energy. Seeking joy after facing adversity is taking back what was stolen from you. When the future is too difficult to imagine, we can find strength by looking to the past" she writes. It is a splendid book rich in lessons and I found it quite helpful in assisting me to build resilience after my own gut-wrenching loss.

Afterward, I also listened as the famed basketball coach Monty Williams (after losing his wife Ingrid) say: ".This will be hard. Things will not get better. But you just can't

give up. You can't give in. God causes all things to work out." He picked up from where she left. I remember during that moment telling myself I can pick up from where Daddy left. I want to pick up from where Japuonj left. I have to pick up from where he left. They had been together with Ingrid for twenty six years and had five kids. At the age of 44, she would be involved in a grisly head on car collision with a woman who had allegedly taken Methamphetamine. She was with three of their kids in the vehicle who escaped with minor injuries. The hand of God, Monty Williams believed, had been kind to him that day only taking one love of his life.

Sports Illustrated contributor Chris Ballard profiled what grieving was like for Monty Williams and in a beautiful paragraph wrote thus:

> "He tries to put the grief in its place, as Pop always advises him to do. Compartmentalize. Still, he sometimes texts her, even though he knows she won't respond. Other times, he looks up, thinking she'll walk around a corner. "I can't say that I feel her presence. I just see so much of her in the kids and so many things remind me of her," Monty says. Sometimes he goes outside and talks to her. "And I don't even know what that's about. I just—I'm not grieving for her, you know. She's in heaven, she's with the Lord, and she's like, balling right now. You grieve because you don't have what you had."

Even the distinguished footballer Rio Ferdinand thinks:

"Grief is the ultimate price of love: and love heals all wounds."

In his documentary, Being Mum and Dad, Rio Ferdinand revealed how the death of his wife Rebecca at only 34 affected him and the kids. "I didn't know what to say to my children, I felt I didn't have the answers for them, but I wanted to know what they were thinking and feeling, I wanted to reach them", he said. In that moving account, he even revealed how he turned into alcohol after the death and that he contemplated suicide, something which he 'never understood previously'. It was an extremely moving documentary due to its sentimentality and openness. Rio Ferdinand also went ahead and co-wrote a book on grief in 2017 with the Award winning journalist Decca Aitkenhead. Decca Aitkenheads' initial book, All At Sea, provides a harrowing account of how her partner Tony Wilkinson drowned in Jamaica while attempting to rescue their young son in 2014.

Rio Ferdinand contends that he wrote the book with the hope that it would help other people who lost someone close find their way through it and surmount the similar difficulties he faced while on the deep end of his grief. The book, Thinking Out Loud: Love, Grief and Being Mum and Dad, packs great punches in unpacking how emotional turmoil and deep loss can become permanent fixtures in our lives if we fail to clutch onto moments of hope. It is actually a courageous digest on loss, love, grief and hope amidst great adversity. If you can, do read it too.

I read endlessly on grief that first year. I would log on to New York Times and type grief on the search bar and then read all the articles that came under. I did this for various reputable websites such as Granta and New Yorker too. I was always reading about loss, and sometimes I bumped into interesting writing about a white lady who had lost a cat or a kid who had lost their dog. Sometimes, it was people who had lost a ring their mother gave them. I learnt grief was different things to different people and that grieving was also not limited to human beings.

I remember reading the timeless 2002 piece by Cheryl Strayed in The Sun titled 'Love of My Life' with great amusement. After losing her mother, Cheryl Strayed had turned to sleeping around and cheating on her husband as a way to deal with the grief. In that story, she details what those sexual escapades meant to her and that she missed her mother with the pinning intensity of sexual love and so she turned to various sexual partners to cure that gap. That is a haunting story I still read with a mix of astonishment and amusement even today.

She poignantly quips:

> 'We are allowed to be deeply into basketball, or Buddhism, or Star Trek or jazz but we are not allowed to be deeply sad. Grief is something that we are encouraged to 'let go of' or 'to move on from' and we are told specifically how

this should be done. Countless well-intentioned friends, distant family members, hospital workers and strangers recounted to me the five stages of grief: denial, anger, bargaining, depression and acceptance.

I did not deny. I did not get angry. I didn't bargain, become depressed or accept. I fucked. I sucked. Not my husband, but people I hardly knew and in that I found a glimmer of relief'.

It is from that article that I remember knowing that I did not have to experience similar motions of grief. It was my journey and it was going to be as personal as it would be paralyzing. Like all manner of pain, grief is an overwhelmingly subjective experience. You clutch at straws hoping you do not drown but you still find yourself drowning at certain times and gasping for air. I contemplated suicide so many times because I thought there was nothing to life anymore. There was never any reason for me to wake up in the morning. I sunk into depression and had endless days that I could not get out of bed and just cried. It was a dark period.

Those days, in my fog of grief, I read unendingly.

Nostalgia: My Fathers Son

In 2014, while still at the peak of my excitement attempting to be a writer, I wrote a blog post on my father that would haunt me after his death.

July 16, 2014

"This morning, my dad sent me airtime worth five hundred shillings. I flinched out of great surprise. It must have been a mistake.

Now, after 21 years, you know your old man pretty well, like you know the location of your mouth while eating in darkness. You know something is up his sleeve just from his actions. After that long time, you know his customary demeanor. When he is irate: and you need to run, or when he is happy: and you need to remind him you need a new pair of trousers. You know he gets cross when supper was Ugali and Omena, and he is wastefully generous after two Tusker beer bottles. How about the fact that he brings home a kilo of goat meat every payday? Ok. Not your dad. Mine neither.

Back to the Manna.

So I decide to call him up to inquire if there was a looting exercise at a Safaricom outlet and he happened to have been at the vicinity. Our archetypal conversations, of late. 'Hey Boss, I happen to receive some airtime on my phone, and it's from your number. Could it be a mistake or what is going on wherever you are?'

'I also have no idea. Why are you calling me again?'

'Not that I plan to return the cash if it's a mistake, but at least I could say sorry before thanking you.'

'Ong'er. (Monkey). You don't call people of late, so I figure your phone doesn't know what credit is anymore. Also buy data and send me your exam results from last semester.'

That is where you hung up the phone. And send a text message claiming a 'network failure' where you presently are. You See, that free airtime had a saddle tied to it. And, yes, my dad still asks for my results at Campus.

But that's not why I decided to write this article. I had decided to do a piece on Father's Day, and then in my characteristic droopy fashion, let it slip by. Ian, kid bro, did a grand piece on the Mzee though. Then I said I would write about him some other day.

Well, here.

Recently, a friend of mine, and classmate, lost his dad. A day after his burial, another classmate and friend lost his dad too. On the same day my dad sent me that manna. Maybe that is what it had to take to let me write on Omondi Wuod Were. That is shit a writer would understand, what makes him write. Sometimes, like now, it is tragedy.

To my Friends, Be Comforted.

I have been thinking so much about my old man of late. About him dying, not today, but whatever time the fiends of death strike. How I would handle it. How the family would handle it. How it feels like to lose a breadwinner. When you lose the man you have looked up to all your life, what kind of mug face do you wake up with the next morning? I don't know if I would have the pluck and fortitude my chums have exhibited this past week. Maybe I would sit in some dingy room at home and do a poem, asking him why he left when I was just becoming a man. Maybe. I don't know. I don't want to find out soon.

I adore my old man. Venerate even. I would choose him for my dad any other day. And I would want him to walk my mum down the aisle again, in the same colorful wedding ceremony as that of 18th December 1998, which remains livid in my memory. The two people I appreciate God the most for. They are breastplates that have held my life together for 21 years now. Or I would have turned out like Otieno Kajwang did. For my political sake, that was me attempting humor.

I loved him when I thought he was mean, when as young kids he was always on his newspaper, never having time for us or never giving us all the attention we were craving for. When our only mode of communication was calling him from the bedroom when food was ready or when he called us to help wipe his shoes. There is something from that haughtiness that buoyed the kid in me. Maybe it was the authority; the macho-ness.

I loved him when he translated from mean to heartless, when he beat me to pulp with a building pole for starting a fire in the house when I was just ten years old. That was my only attempt at being superman, which ended up with a sore and stinging ass. The only time my father made me lie down and gave me some serious flogging. The only time he ever used violence on me, taking note of the fact that he was a teacher who flogged his students all the time.

I loved him when I realized he was a human after all,

which is when he bought us those priceless BMX bikes for acing exams. For the record, we had it first, before other kids in our area joined the bandwagon: and boy we had the bragging rights in the hood.

I loved this clueless and dense man who visited me at boarding school in primary six with only a newspaper, again and again. Then when later in High School he learnt, like other kids, I could also do with fried chicken on school visiting days. Oh, and I love how he makes his chicken, this old fogey of ours.

But I hated his old ramshackle Peugeot, KAP 017K. Decrepit would not even begin to describe it. And it was yellow. An old yellow Peugeot, in 2003, after the Millennium, was hot fodder for embarrassment. But the bloke loved that 'machine' like he had given up the world to have it. We saw him practice driving at the field using it, and we thought maybe it was just being used to train an amateur. Then one day it landed home, and stayed there for a while. Within no time, a structure was coming up to house it. And the rest became history, because we had to live with it. Honestly, I became fond of it later though. After a lot of press-ganging and arm twisting however, he gave in, and changed the color to white.

Still.

But nothing made me hate him like when he made me repeat standard seven. I had been in the Crème de la

Crème at my former school when I joined this boarding
School. Then due to culture shock, I flunked all my
exams that first year. So he made me repeat the class,
and lost touch with all the friends I had made. Honestly,
I am yet to reconnect with most of them. Looking back,
nonetheless, I should have appreciated him. Clichéd
though, I would not have been here today. Benefit of
hindsight. And I got so happy when he went to pick my
calling letter and told me, over the phone, that I was
going to Maranda. I said a Hail Mary.

Senior Thomas Omondi Were is not the conventional
dad though. Hates Nairobi to its core, and would rather
work somewhere in the middle of Alfred Mutuas phony
road. He stopped buying us Christmas clothes when we
stopped wetting the bed. Has no time for scolding, and
when wrong, only looks at you with a smile that says 'Try-
Me-Not'.

Like all our fathers, grew up in so much struggle. You
should see him glorifying how walking to school barefoot
made him the man. He want to high school in akala:
sandals made from car tires. And then wait to be called
Ong'er. Ha-ha. That High School bed of his that was made
of reeds carried from home is what makes me cringe
though. Dude struggled his way up.

Running towards old age like a bull on heat, I marvel at
how he remains inspired. Recently, while gobbling down
Kuku he had paid for at Ranalo Foods with kid bro, he

asked us what time we wake up. I am glad you don't
expect anything before 10am. And went on to rant about
how all successful men wake up earlier than the rest, to
read. On reading part I was off the hook though. It keeps
me sane.

How about our first time at a bar, when I attempted to
order a beer and he insisted on a soda, that 'you do not
drink a beer when you cannot afford to buy yourself one'.
To date, I love it when I buy my own beer.

I never forget how he once tried his hands in large scale
Passion Fruit farming, and it was a flop. Ok, we ate most
of the fruits and he reacted like it was nothing when it
all failed, like it was just a phase in his journey to the top.
And nowadays, our conversations are shaped on Success.
What do you think about Chicken Farming? Which shares
sell most at the moment? For him, the future is on the tip
of his nose. His wishes, should he go before achieving
them, I will fulfill them. Don't they say men simply try to
be a better version of their dads?

It is my success that I want the old man to be around
to see. I want him to see that I amounted to something.
That he inspired me to be a better man, dad and husband.
I want to one day visit him at his home in Masiro, with
grey hair, and hear him say he is ready to die, because he
leaves a proficient man behind. I want him to be swollen
with pride every day of his old life. Otherwise I would
have become a DJ.

In his old age, I want to buy him old Chilean wine and quadruple distilled Irish whisky, and watch him fumble in disgust wondering what they are: because in those grey days, as he shits on his pants, drunk, I want to be my father's son."

It was quite the cheesy article an excited first year writes when he is just learning the ropes of the craft of writing.

I remember how he took issue with that article because he ended up reading it. Up to then, I had not realized that my father read any of my articles. He never said anything. So it was a surprise to me when I woke up the next day to a long ass comment from him that I had to delete almost half of before sending it out. He took issue with the fact that 18th December 1998 was not their wedding date. He said his fast car was not a Peugeot but a Datsun and he loved it to death. He asked me how you would claim to love someone and still call them dense. He must have Googled dense and took the first meaning Google threw at him. I had not expected him to read the article as I had also embellished some facts in the story. He deadass caught me flatfooted.

It was very sad to me that the man could not stick around to even see me graduate from Law School at the end of 2017. That's why this 2014 piece largely haunted me at that moment. I regret that my father did not see me succeed in anything meaningful: that he could not wait for just seven months to see me graduate from the

University. In point of fact, my father had loaned me 25000/= to go begin life in Nairobi and asked me to pay it back immediately. He did not stay around to even eat a cent from my sweat after all the work he had put in to ensure I had had the best life he could have offered me. He did not fucking eat a cent from me. I am gutted he could not wait to have me buy him an expensive Chilean Wine and Scottish Whiskey in his sunset years.

Without my father, I know my success will haunt me for the rest of my life. I know every damn time I will achieve a milestone it will be a bittersweet moment for me because he would not be there to see it. I cannot imagine anybody else who would have been immensely proud of the milestones I am about to unlock in my life like my father would have. Silently, I knew he was always cheering me on and I knew he always believed in me and I have always been keen of making him really proud. I wanted to make him the proudest man in the village and I wanted him to have a smile on his face every damn time my name would be mentioned. It was something I always thought about when I was unable to sleep. After my father's death and for almost two years, I lost he will to live and I hope to one day get the courage to share that story too.

For which man does not strive to be a better version of his father.

After his death, I remember how my mind kept flashing

to my entire life. I had a very simple life growing up. In our household, there was never any sort of largesse or pretentious posturing. As I have narrated elsewhere in this book, my parents struggled to ensure that we had the best life they could guarantee us. I actually think as a result we had a pretty content life growing up because we wanted very simple things and we never lacked them. I remember when we needed a bike and all we had to do for it was perform well in class. Or when I needed a phone when I completed Standard 8 and all my father had to do was go pick from one of the phones he had confiscated from one of his High School students. We even had new 'Christmas Clothes' all through our childhood. In fact, the festivities were always my favorite time of the year because my father always hired a pick-up truck and bundled us in it and off we all went to spend time in the village. I lived for those days.

On the bike incident, I remember his promise in Standard Four that if I would become among the best five students, he would buy me the BMX bike. It was the craze of our time and I wanted to own one by all means. I had never been among the best five but that term I managed to become third after only Marvin Ooko and Eric Wambedha. The next day after I handed him my report form, he went to Kisumu and came back with a yellow BMX bike and handed it to me, but said I could share with Ian because he had also performed well but he could only buy one bike.

That bike shot my street credits to stratospheric levels in that small tight knit community of 'watoto wa walimu' we had somehow built at Rang'ala. I used it to finally flex my muscles because even the girls were now noticing me. I remember that is the first time I got close to Akinyi, who was the most beautiful girl in the area. I grew very close to her as I taught her how to ride: an experience that would be cut short a little later because her mother would end up buying a similar bike for her. I flexed with the boys because they were constantly asking for riding time and it would always depend on my mood. Heck, I even flexed with Ian despite the fact that the bike was to be co-owned in a way.

That bike incident taught me that my father kept his promises and indeed he did keep all his promises to me until he passed on.

Anyway, a year after buying me the bike, out of excitement, I would walk into the house with a burning piece of paper and stumble into my father in the sitting room. He had not been around and I had wanted to scare my brothers that I could burn them if they joked. He simply told me to go throw the paper outside and come back with a cane. Before that moment, my father had never beaten me and so I had taken it with a pinch of salt and gone back to playing outside. Later in the evening as I would come back to the house for evening porridge, I would find him calmly seated with a massive cane that was the size of a hockey stick. What happened

next was terror. I think he had forgotten I was not one of his Form Four students at School. That would be the first and last time my father would raise his hands on me: but to also credit myself, nothing would warrant such a beating ever again. From that day, I always approached him with very great caution and our relationship was always built on fear from that day until when I was fully becoming anadult did the real fear actually dissipate.

In 2006, my father decided that we would both be taken to boarding school with Ian. The resident parish priest Father Clement had suggested we go to Father Schaeffer Boys in Asumbi instead of Ndere Boys that we were initially set to join. So, on 12th January 2006, we bundled ourselves into the Fathers car and headed for Asumbi. I cannot describe how I felt at that time but I know there was a tinge of excitement because I thought I was always going to be independent from there on but I also felt the fear of leaving my comfort zone. See, I had always been among the best students at Rang'ala Boys Primary School and I lived literally five minutes from school so I usually sneaked home for snacks during any of the breaks. This was going to be no walk in the park.

I have a lot of memories of my father from this journey. I remember how we stopped for lunch at Kisii and he assured me that would be the best lunch I would eat in a while so I should eat to my fill and I thought he was bluffing. How bad could the food at a boarding school be? Well, I would later come to learn the word

unpalatable to describe food. He then assured me that it was now time to become a man and that I should continue doing well in School and taking my studies seriously. We took the journey to Scheffer and when he left me there that day; I came to terms with the reality that I had been dumped in a lion's cage because that school was a detention camp.

That first year, I performed very poorly, often blaming it on the culture shock when he asked me. I was consistently among the last three and so at the end of the year my dad would be called to make a decision on if I should proceed or repeat. I have never forgotten how he pulled me aside, told me he would plead for me to go to the next class but I would be given a pass mark of 250 which if I failed to achieve then I would have to repeat Standard 7. He convinced the Head teacher and that is how I landed in Standard 8 the next year for one month before getting 212 marks and my ass being bundled back to the lower class.

The one time my father flat out lied to me and maybe for a good reason was when I failed to get a National School after scoring impressive results in my KCSE. I had been called to Maranda High School and I had felt that the school had no name when I compared it to my choice of Alliance High School. We had been competing for entry into Alliance High School with Zephaniah Adar and he had ended up getting the school so I knew my chances were already up in smoke but I was willing to

compromise and join Maseno School. Today, I know my father felt Maseno was above my abilities but he did not tell me at that point. He told me he would get me into Maseno and he had already starterd the process but it is my offer letter that was delayed so he asked me to go to Maranda just for one term and then begin my study at Maseno the following term. Maseno School never materialized and I ended up studying the whole of High school at Maranda: to which I have no regrets because I was in the 'Maranda Invincibles' class of 2011. I however only forgave him after I got my A from Maranda.

At Maranda, my father visited me a few times when my mother could not make it. He often tried to live up to how my mother came for the visiting but he could not. Instead of cooked food, he carried snacks and instead of doing adequate shopping, he carried money instead for me to do the shopping at the school canteen. I always insisted on my mum being the one to come and he only came on days my mother could not make it in any circumstance. A few times, they came together and those were my best visiting days in school. I have always loved my parents and I am always forever grateful for them sticking out despite the obvious problems that sometimes came to the fore. I know they stuck their thumbs out for us and nothing else.

All his life, I saw my father lead. I remember coming of age when my father had already been made the Principal of Rang'ala Boys Secondary School taking over from Mr.

Ohonde who had been such a big deal. There had been some complaints from certain quarters admonishing Ohonde for trusting his legacy with the meek quiet man who ended up leading the school for close to ten years and who distinguished himself as a performer. He would be fondly referred to as 'Omosh' and students who knew me referred to me as 'Wuod Omosh' whenever I passed by the playing field. I remember during the requiem mass at Kisumu, Father Oscar who had been one of his students recalled how my father would issue you with a suspension letter while smiling and I perfectly remembered those Rang'ala days. Those were some really glorious days too. I am awed at how my father ensured we remained down to earth despite being watoto wa mkubwa. There was never any sort of hubris in our house.

I am also reminded of an incidence I knew I was always going to ask my father about in later years. On the night after we buried my grandfather, we had a discotheque at home and I got quite drunk. Since there was such a large crowd, I knew I would lose my phone if I did not keep it but there was no right way to keep it coming to mind so I walked to my father and handed it to him. We had a short conversation and I don't remember what it was about at all. I know he realized I was quite soiled. The next day when I picked the phone from him he said nothing. It is only my mother, while being a tad dramatic; who while on our journey back brought up the conversation in the car and asked why we were becoming alcoholics at such a young age. My father, he just kept quiet and drove.

What was he thinking?

What was he always thinking?

Gratitude

Father's Day is typically not a big deal all over the world. It is like Jay Pritchett says in Modern Family the dirty step-child of holidays. We grow up knowing that thinking too much about such holidays is emasculating. We grow up assured that celebrating the men that our fathers have been to us is being weak because that is primarily their foremost responsibility. As a man, there is no achievement in showing up: it is supposed to be a definite. Heck, we even grow up knowing that celebrating our own selves is emasculating because men are born to be macho. So such holidays, as opposed to Mother's Day or the International Womens Day, pass by without much revel. In most cases, they pass by without any fuss. On the same day, the World Toilet day is celebrated.

The best we get to do is probably jot down a Facebook post which again is mostly done by the girl child, couching it as "celebrating the men in their lives". As boys we just watch from a distance out of the fear of being weakened and knowing fully well that in the same vein our fathers do not expect anything from us. There is therefore a sort of an unwritten concession that that holiday is unnecessary.

I only remember becoming so conscious about the role my father had played in my life when I completed High School. After eighteen years, I knew what it meant to for instance have a father who was simply present. I had seen how most of my friends who had grown without their fathers had turned out. Mostly I just took it for granted, but growing without a father had wrecked a couple of my friends and they hadn't even realized it themselves. I had seen what growing without a father who was merely present could do. I had also seen how growing with a father had been quite impactful in the lives of my other relations. Fathers were meant to be an always present line of defence.

So I was really proud I had a great father, and I wanted to grow up to be the kind of present father he was. He was always my compass on family values. I saw him every day when I was home and I took that as an indicator of the sort of man he was, of course looking at things then from a very simplistic angle. I knew how rare it was to have a father who came back home every evening, irrespective of what else he did.

On the Father's Day of 2012 therefore, I knew I wanted to appreciate my father. I was only nineteen years old so I was racking my head on what I would do that would show my father I celebrated him. I had no money so there was nowhere I was going to take him for lunch, and even if I had had the money, I would not have taken him for lunch because he would have asked me where I actually got the money from in the first place and that would have ruined the whole thing. Also, the little money I had I always used to impress my girlfriend who unfortunately ended up leaving me that Christmas and got knocked up. All is fair in love and war.

I had an idea and so after brainstorming with my best friend Theodore, we came up with a plan where I was going to text his father that his son loved and appreciated him and he was going to do the same to my father. We were going to do that simultaneously so that the two gentlemen would receive the same message at the same time. I do not know why we thought that was such a cool thing to do. So I took out my phone and texted Juma Zaddock telling him "he was a great father and he had a great son". I told him 'we celebrate him this Father's Day with Theodore and Theodore loves him greatly".

He did the same.

I had been seated near my father in a bid to see his reaction and I saw him look at the phone, smile amusingly before replying to the message. My father would then call him to say "thank you" as we sat watching news. J.Z as we fondly called him would do the same later that evening.

That was a genius idea, we seemed quite sure and we pulled it off.

Every Father's Day after that, I always told him he was a great dad. I made sure he knew I appreciated the much he had done for me. I wrote to him long WhatsApp messages. I made sure I assured him he had taught me every great lesson I held dear. I made sure I told him 'I love you, Daddy' every single time for the six years before he passed on. But only on Father's Day. That 2012 momentum we began with Theo had acted as my push. I do not think I would have followed with the messages the subsequent years if there had been no reply to the first one.

That is why the one person I celebrate so much today (and for the rest of time) is Theodore Juma. I know he deserves to hog this gratitude section. Between us, there is a solid ten years of friendship today that has weathered whatever storms friendships weather. We have been great friends since our high school days when we were young and excited form one students at Maranda High School. We had been desk mates since our first term in high school and that only changed from Form Three when I went a step behind to sit with Brian Ogenya and Brian Obura took up my spot.

Like with every friendship, we have had the usual bad days and good days as friends but we have stuck it out. Together with Brian Ogenya, we formed a trio

we christened "The Three Musketeers" in High School which has been the great badge of our friendship. These two guys have been the greatest shoulders I have had to lean on. On countless times when I was at my worst, Brian and Theo have come through for me in ways I do not think I would be able to repay them. A few months after my dad passed on, they took me and Ian for a road trip with some of our closest friends and it was a great juncture for our friendship that I am forever grateful for.

Theodore is an easy, dog-eared guy. I have always wanted to describe him as dog-eared. Says very little, but brilliant to a fault. Amongst the Musketeers, he is the laid back relaxed dude. He is the predictable sit on the fence guy who doesn't take sides often. I had a falling out with Brian, and he has learnt to sit on the balance ledge without taking sides. The two gentlemen have been good to me. I am the noise maker, the one who does all the talking and mostly, the one who gets most of the shit done. I am the volatile Musketeer bomb. I like to say I am Aranos. I organize the road trips and the parties and sometimes just coming together. I am a believer in memento mori and I believe relationships should last until they can't anymore but if this friendship should end, it has been a scream.

During the stretch my father was in hospital though, Theodore turned into a personal doctor of sorts. I was always so desperate I constantly doubted every move the nurses or the doctor made in treating my father.

"Is this how they should do it?"

"What is the function of an ultrasound?"

"What do you think about the doctor saying he should be injected with this?"

"What is the function of these tablets?"

"They say they could not see anything from the Computerized Tomography Scan. Isn't that where they see Cancer cells?"

"What the fuck is going on here Chief?"

I had unending questions and Theodore would patiently handle them one by one even if sometimes I always became a little bit overzealous or annoying. He was kind enough to me. Some days he would call or text to ask his own questions with great concern

"Did he eat?"

"What nutrients are they feeding him with?"

"How slow are those people yawa?"

"What tests have they done today?'

I know I had never been this desperate in my life. And here was the one person who despite not having gone through the same, was helping me handle it. I can say for a fact that Theodore was the only one person who when he asked "How is he today?' I never answered with the usual 'Its fine'. Because I could tell him he was not fine and he was not going to be hollow about it. He did not expect me to be superficial with him even if he could only do so much.

I remember the day he told me that this liver issue that was not being found out could have been a "Budd-Chiari Syndrome" and I approached the doctor with it and he laughed at me saying I could not even spell Budd-Chiari in the first place, so how did I come to know about it. I still don't know if that is the spelling of that word. He went ahead to investigate if it could have been a possibility and it wasn't, and then he told me I would have made a great doctor from how I had constantly pressed him whenever I had my doubts. I know I may not be able to repay Theodore for the kindness he showed me on that day and several many days and months after I lost my father but I hope God pays him back in a great way. If you should read this, thank you for the friendship.

Ricky Thomas Nyakach one evening passed by to see my father in hospital and he remains the only of my friends who would manage to visit at the hospital. I have also known Nyakach for a very long time and he has been good to me in the most selfless of ways. Our friendship has had several twists in between but we have always managed to stay true to each other and I turned to Nyakach several times when my dad had passed on and not one time did he turn his back on me. Ricky is my best friend today because there is nothing in this world we have not gone through together and emerged on the other side. When my father passed on, and till this day, I know I can count on Nyakach on those days I need a hand. The third Musketeer in this friendship is Innocent Ngare, a friend who has since turned to family and who I love to death too and who will not shy away from getting me a bottle of whiskey and telling me to take my pain in stride because bad things happen to good people all the time.

I had not imagined how many of my friends would make it for the burial and it was a surprise when I saw everybody there. Brenda Ogenya, Ivy Kabuthu, Peter Ojare, Elvince Ager, Dick Okite, Innocent Omollo, Angela Ogutu, Angie Oloo, Jackvine Omingo, Lizzah Aquilliah, Irvin Jalang'o, Brian Ogenya, Theodore Juma, Erick Wambedha, Peter Odemba, Ricky Thomas, Dan Odemba and Yvonne Aprils just to mention a few. It was a whole parade of my friends and I realized I had a really great team behind me.I have always not taken it for granted since that day over the people who were there to help me bury my father. I hope when these people ever need me one day in their lives, I will be able to cross oceans for them. I know there is very little it would take me to not come through for these guys.

I am forever grateful to everybody who stood with us

as a family and continue to stand by us. My uncle Mark Keya has remained a towering father figure to me to this day. And so are my paternal uncles Peter, Hillary, Richard and Julian and all my aunts. I would be remiss if I did not thank the KSSHA-Siaya team. I have great cousins with whom we continue to hold each other's hands and so Victor, Moses, Kevin, Hesborn and all my cousins this is a heartfelt shout out. It has been a harrowing period for our family losing my dad and my grandparents in the short span of three years. Even when we lost my grandmother during the corona virus crisis, it is still the same names that came through. I am happy I can say that when tragedy visited my family, there are strong shoulders we were able to lean on and I am forever indebted to these giants.

This has been the rockiest stretch of our lives as the entire Were family, but better days must surely lie ahead. We must keep dancing with our banged up hearts. Our turn at the lever is yonder and I know we cannot give up now. I am personally forever grateful for the support that I have received from the extended family as a whole and even if I was to write another book, I would never do the indebtedness justice. I hope we all continue to live out the legacy of the three shining lights we have lost in the unfortunate quick succession over the three year period.

Our heads have to remain on top of the water.

Epilogue

Two days after burying my father, we sat by the foyer of his house trying to come to terms with what our reality was going to be moving forward. Things were looking quite gloomy and yet at the same time we knew there was no alternative to a forward march. I remember telling my family I was going to write a book and getting no reaction: probably because by that time I had said I would do a lot of things and not come through on them. Top on the list was buying my mum a car, of which I was already four months late as I babbled endlessly about writing a book. I actually asked my sister if her employer, Oxford Publishing House, would publish a memoir and she retorted with an emphatic NO. I did not bother to ask if it was a No because their publishing house would not touch my manuscript or she was flat out just shutting me up out of needless excitement: it did not matter. I was hell-bent on writing this book, and I assured them it would take me only six months to do so. It ended up taking three years and I know this will nonetheless still come as a surprise to most of them that I followed

through with writing this book.

Writing this book has been a labour of love. There are days I enjoyed writing it and other long stretches of time that I hated the process for one reason or another. There are long periods of time I went without writing a single word because I actually doubted I had anything to say let alone write about losing my father. I gave up several times and it is Ricky Thomas who would jolt me with a "Where is the book you've been writing?"

I knew people I considered better writers who had lost their parents and not written a book and so there are days I never believed I would complete a manuscript detailing my stretch of pain. There are also large swathes of pages and paragraphs I deleted because I felt they were not saying what I wanted to say despite painstakingly coming up with them over a long period of staggered writing.

It was laborious and hard even coming up with individual chapters but I knew I had to, at least for once in my life, finish what I had started. This was going to be my pet project and a lesson on discipline, and I knew I had to follow through with it. I wanted to share what losing my father was like and how grief was like being bundled into a dark tunnel and being asked to find your way out. It was like walking around with a permanent bag of cement affixed on my shoulder and still knowing life had to move on. Things were never going to be the same, but there was always going to be room for more things.

I hope dear reader that you have found certain tidbits from this book that you can use for your life or your writing. I hope I have done justice telling the story of a man I greatly adored and loved and whom losing felt like an Armageddon to me. I was always aware that telling this story was a burden I had to bear. I have tried to do so. Do you not know that a man is not dead while his name is still spoken? Terry Pratchett asks. This is an attempt to keep the legacy of my father forever. This is an attempt to ensure his great life is not erased as the years go by. This is for my father. This is for a loss I had to bear too soon.

I also attempt to share my story of grief in this book as a cathartic experience for me: because on days I could not leave bed, all I could do was read and write. It gave me sanity and I hope reading this book gives a person going through a similar experience some semblance of sanity too. I hope the parallels of our experiences assure you of your survival too. I hope the times you read this book it did numb your grief. With their numbered days, those we have lost gave us great hope in our lives, and we can continue to walk with that hope in our hearts. It eventually does get better, I can finally write so.

They existed, and that will forever never change however scarred our souls may be. I hope we all get to learn that there is no shame in holding onto our grief; all

we have to do is ensure we make room for everything else too, and we continue to live our lives to the fullest. It is Sylvan Kamens who said that at the blueness of the skies and in the warmth of the summer, we must always remember those we have lost. I will forever remember my grandparents and the grace with which they lived their lives.

I will always honor my father.

So long, Daddy.

So very long.

THE END

www.ingramcontent.com/pod-product-compliance
Lightning Source LLC
Chambersburg PA
CBHW051959150726
47999CB00004B/1449